Make life Your Favorite
ADVENTURE

Zone of Potential

Karin Schultz

DEDICATION

I dedicate this book to

my mother
Charlotte
for her gracious, resourceful, accepting ways

my father
Werner (Fritz)
for his strength, courage, resilience

my brothers and sisters,
Werner (Rocky), Erika, Heidi, Rob, Kris, and Alex
for a childhood filled with amazing ADVENTURES

AND

my daughter,
Amanda
for my most incredible ADVENTURE of a lifetime

Foreword

*A*dventure! The word even sounds exhilarating. While adventure may suggest excitement to some, it invokes apprehension in others. Our entire lives are adventures and should be full of anticipation and excitement. Yet all too often we find ourselves stuck or frozen. We want something different. Although we may have to make uncomfortable decisions, it is within each choice where the adventure begins.

To know Karin is, in and of itself, an adventure. Her animated style and colorful expressions are evident in her coaching techniques. In this book, Karin incorporates some stories of wonderful people along with her own to share what most people experience when navigating unpredictable waters of life. She applies her "ADVENTURE" guide to make sense of these real-life stories so we may use them in our own and help get us "unstuck from the muck".

As one of Karin's first clients, I was introduced early to her unique concept of ADVENTURE. You see, I was at a crossroad trying to make career and lifestyle decisions. In order to make the "right" choice, I wanted to consider everyone and everything. Karin showed me how to unpack the entire gift of who I am and how I can use my past to forge my future by defining what is most important to me. As we applied the ADVENTURE model, I uncovered underlying things about myself along with long-forgotten passions and desires I had for my future. While we reflected on the past and explored the possibilities of the future, I not only learned more about myself, I actually became more excited about the possibilities in the road ahead.

In keeping with her military background, Karin frequently uses acronyms for ease in remembering and to quickly cut through lengthy descriptions. ADVENTURE is no exception. She will *Awaken* you and *Dance* with you as you *Venture* and *Embrace* your newly discovered direction. She will remind you to *Nurture* yourself and your surroundings and *Thank* yourself and others for hidden treasures of past, present and future experiences. She will show you how to *Uplift* yourself and others within your sphere of influence. You will learn to be more **Resilient** by aligning your values and strengths while accepting the support of others to help you be your best you. And finally, among many other of words she could have chosen, Karin decided to bless you with **Enjoy** because, after all, that is what we seek in life and any adventure.

Life is an adventure and filled with mystery. This book is useful in all areas of life not limited to: goal setting, career, personal relationships, family, fitness, retirement, and the list goes on. Come on the journey with Karin; playfully and purposefully perfecting your dance. You will find that you are not where you used to be and, most likely, be where you never thought you could.   *~Erika Zinkan~*

A Short Note to Reader

*A*s delighted as I am to bring forth this creation, I am also aware that people are on different paths and navigate them at their own pace. We all have our own beliefs and ideals about how life should be lived. I do not claim to know or fully understand the depth or breadth of your life's circumstances. But, if a deeper appreciation of your life is what you seek, *Zone of Potential* can help reveal many aspects of it. What you unveil about yourself from the contents can empower you to decide what is best for your situation and create the life you desire.

Although you can read *Zone of Potential* from start to finish, sometimes you might need just a slice to nudge you. Each chapter contains ideas and concepts, universal laws, quick snippets, and maybe even a story for you to consider. As you employ any of these tools, you may find it difficult at first and notice cascading effects in other areas of your life. You may experience reactions or responses from things in your immediate surroundings and levels of transformation, some abrupt and others gradual. Each decision you make will require a level of scrutiny before acting. Do your best to remember that what works for one does not work for all. Use your inner wisdom to choose wisely.

Abundance, prosperity, and freedom extend beyond the material world and reside within each of us. We simply need to recognize that we have the power to access our magnetism and experience it whenever we choose. You deserve a life filled with peace, joy, and love. If this is what you seek, the words contained within *Zone of Potential* can be your guide along the path. I am forever grateful and humbled to share this opportunity. I wish you tremendous success on your journey to make life your favorite ADVENTURE!

Table of Contents

Acknowledgements 9

Zone of Potential 11

    Zone Fundamentals 13

    ADVENTURE Barriers 20

    The ADVENTURE Guide 22

AWAKEN 23

    I Am 23

    I Value 26

    I Do 30

    I Will 34

DANCE 43

    Talented You 43

    Knowledge 44

    Skills 47

    Finesse 49

VENTURE 57

    The Big Picture 58

    SWOT It 67

    Start Small 71

    Jumping In 77

EMBRACE 85

    Looking Back 86

    Life's Wonderful Gifts 93

    Presents in Presence 98

    Gift of Interior Design 102

NURTURE 109

    Be Healthy 109

    Be Well 116

    Be Kind 122

Be Gentle 127

THANK 133

Gratitude in Lessons 133

Fortunes in Forgiveness 137

Grateful Creations 141

A Future to Appreciate 147

UPLIFT 151

Reflections of You 152

Manage Your Inner Critic 154

Critics on the Outside 155

Criticisms of Errors 157

RESILIENT 165

Commit or Quit 165

Feedback not Fail 174

Resource or Resign 181

Flow or Force 190

ENJOY 199

ENJOY Happiness Within 199

ENJOY Being Love 201

ENJOY Being Joy 203

ENJOY Being PEACE 205

Make Life Your Favorite ADVENTURE 213

A Special Tribute to Walter Darring 224

Acknowledgements

I believe that nothing done well and with heartfelt meaning is done alone. This book writing ADVENTURE was nothing short of a collective effort of support and wisdom. Those acknowledge below offered me encouragement, support, and guidance, yet they are merely a fraction of so many others, who inspired me along the way.

To my friends and associates who encouraged me, along with family members in the dedication, thank you for the gentle nudges, words of strength, and confirmation that this information will help so many. A special thanks to:

John Boken, Forever Groom and Best Friend
Cynthia Davis, Business/Personal Growth Coach and Author
Chyna Mae, Graphic Designer and Cover Artist
Elizabeth Duncan-Hawker, Author, Speaker, and Accountability buddy
Alice Hoey, Professor and Developmental Editor
Kelly Falardeau, Publishing Partner, Author, Speaker
Carol Everly, Editor and Neighbor

Thanks also to my family, friends, and colleagues who supported me. Your gifts of self are what made the material in *Zone of Potential* come to life and relatable. A special thank you to Uncle Walt/Sonny and children for authorizing his tribute and the use of his artwork and to those who shared their stories sprinkled throughout the book. And finally, to Jessie, my elderly blind doggy who endured long walks and guided me in managing my energy.

Finally, to all masters, authors, and speakers not listed above who came before me or are here today! Thanks for your knowledge, wisdom, and inspiration that guided me along and influenced me to bring about *Zone of Potential.*

US Anderson, Ken Blanchard, Gregg Braden, Marcus Buckingham, Dolores Cannon, Edgar Cayce, Deepak Chopra, Russell Conwell, Stephen R. Covey, Ram Dass, John Demartini, Joe Dispenza, Wayne Dyer, Sigmund Freud, Neville Goddard, David Hawkins, Abraham Hicks, Napoleon Hill, Adriana James, Tad James, Carl Jung, Michio Kaku, Bruce Lipton, Michael Losier, John Maxwell, Tricia McCannon, Drunvalo Melchizedek, Joseph Murphy, Earl Nightingale, Bob Proctor, Jim Rohn, Eckhart Tolle, Iyanla Vanzant, Joe Vitale, Wallace Wattles, Alan Watts, Vadim Zeland, and so many others!

Knowledge is valuable only if used and shared with others to create a powerful positive impact on the world.

Zone of Potential

Make life Your Favorite
ADVENTURE

Zone of Potential

*E*ach of us is on a quest to figure out who we are and what we are here to do. Although we have similar basic needs, our wants and paths to achieve them are unique. Some of us have desires aligned with our upbringing, culture, heritage, religion, and several other factors. Others move away from their childhood in search of something new. As we look outside of ourselves today to validate old beliefs of our past, we may even try on new ones to get us closer to our own truths. In the long run, if we are not satisfied or experiencing what we want, our endeavors can prove to be frustrating and confusing.

Ultimately, each one of us holds the keys to our innermost desires. We are called to tap into these keys and use them to live a life of ADVENTURE. *Imagine* what it would be like if you looked at your life a little differently. *Imagine* living with a sense of ADVENTURE where the risk to reward could never be wrong or bad. *Imagine* if you considered your life an ADVENTURE novel where you create what happens. *Imagine* letting go of expectations and responding with flexibility, curiosity, and excitement. This is what you do in your *Zone of Potential*.

Our approaches to doing so are as individual as we are. With that in mind, as you read through this and following chapters, remember you have the ability to create who you want to be, what you want to do, and what you want to have, however you can imagine it. You are the author and orchestrator of your life!

Your *Zone of Potential* is where everything happens for you. It's where you choose your pathways and ADVENTURES to fulfill your purpose and give your life meaning. When we do not choose wisely, we can get lost on our journey and stripped of our identities along the way. The disoriented effect can devastate our lives and those who love us the most. Instead of a life of family, friends, and fun, we find ourselves lonely while wondering what happened and who we are supposed to be.

I'd like to propose that we are more than our mere identities. Ultimately, you are a beautiful soul on a mission to learn, create, teach, and master lessons that aid in your evolution. To support you along the way, you've been gifted with an intelligent body that functions and repairs itself in many ways on its own. No matter how your body physically came into existence or what it looks like today, it is perfectly formed to carry out your specific mission. As you grow and discover more about yourself, you'll see that everything exists and happens for a reason. When you understand these reasons, you reveal who you indeed are and therefore, your purpose! Here is where the ADVENTURE guidelines come into play.

Implementing the ADVENTURE principles lead to a more balanced approach to life. Each letter within ADVENTURE describes aspects of your existence and contributes to a life filled with purpose and meaning. By using the guiding principles of ADVENTURE, you will AWAKEN to who you are and soon see that you are right where you're supposed to be. You will discover your DANCE and begin to VENTURE onto new pathways with enthusiasm and courage. Along the way, you will EMBRACE who and where you are and find joy in your efforts to NURTURE yourself and everything you value. You will discover the power in gratitude as you offer THANKS for all of your experiences, past, present, and those yet to come. Your beauty and radiance will shine bright as you UPLIFT yourself and others. You will find strength

#66 the eyeful tower – what you see is not always as it seems. Each floor tells a different story of your life. You have the power to design it any way you want.

in your power to choose and create the support necessary for you to be RESILIENT and stay the course. Above all, you will learn to ENJOY the happiness, love, joy, and peace that life has to offer. Throughout the chapters, each word is capitalized as a reminder, that from alpha to omega, your life is a series of ADVENTURES, beginning to end.

Even though the principles sound easy, in reality we must be willing to put forth effort toward areas where we struggle. The key challenges we may face are the reluctance to EMBRACE our short-comings, natural discomfort with change, uncertainty of how to transform, and the feeling of overwhelm about where to start. Additionally, because life events are so vast and cascading, we can become stunned by the enormity of the challenge. Instead of designing a meaningful life of value and joy, we fall in line with our old actions and create the same dull and uninspiring expected results. We ignore our creative abilities to make conscious, wise choices, and we get nowhere. It doesn't have to be that way. You have the power of imagination and choice to do what you want! It's in your *Zone of Potential* where all of that happens.

The central message of ADVENTURE is for you to let go of the anxiety associated with being right or wrong and good or bad. ADVENTURES are your opportunities to learn and grow. Through your development, they are to create value and joy in your life and bring the same to those you encounter. They also allow you opportunities to teach others so they can pick up the lead and enable you to move closer to your own mastery. At mastery, you know you've carried your ADVENTURE through to the end.

Law of Conscious Detachment or Non-Attachment - Separate meaning from your experiences and accept the reality of them for what they are. Your resistance to what is creates problems. Enjoy all positivity and allow negativity to flow through you.

Zone Fundamentals

You are always in your *Zone of Potential*. What you do there is up to you! You have the freedom to decide who you want to be, how you want to think and feel, what you want to do, and how you want to do it. Within your Zone, you have many pathways, each containing its own ADVENTURES. As you move along your pathways, each allows you opportunities to tap into your purest potential and develop mastery. In all actuality, you have the power to choose how far you want to go in each ADVENTURE!

Freedom of Choice

A beautiful part about being a human, and even more so a human adult, is we have the power to choose. You get to decide what you want to do, when you want to do it, and who you want to bring with you on your journey in life. Although other things, people, and events also exist, they will not necessarily enter your conscious world unless you give them attention and meaning. Choose wisely!

We often hear people say they didn't have a choice or they only had a couple of options. We all know there is not a lot of truth in those statements. We also know people who remain stuck in circumstances that wreak havoc on their lives as they struggle to find a way out. What they do not realize is, in their *Zone of Potential*, they can consciously choose their state of mind, how they behave, and what they do. It's up to each one of us to decide the life we desire that works for us and allows us to be what we want to be. You don't have to continue down the same path. You can choose something different and make an ADVENTURE out of it. It's that simple!

Every one of our choices is very subjective and determined by, not only where we are now, but the desire and drive we have to pursue it. Your greatest ADVENTURE is the one that not only brings you value and joy but also positively impacts others. As you get a taste of this true freedom of choice, you will open your world to limitless possibilities and work toward your purest potential.

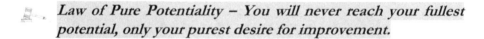

Law of Pure Potentiality – You will never reach your fullest potential, only your purest desire for improvement.

Pure Potential

As you navigate your *Zone of Potential*, know that you have limitless possibilities and will never reach your fullest potential. The reason is because you can always develop in some new way. When you think about it, someone always seems to know a little more or do a little better than we do. That's okay; do not get hung up on that. They are on their path in their Zone. Instead, concentrate on reaching your **purest** potential. This pureness is your highest achievement based on intent and your willingness to go after what you want. Once you've shifted focus or priorities, you'll find your old potential in that area will naturally fade, but you'll take your talents with you on your next path. It's necessary and integral to your development. Think of it this way; each place you land is your next new beginning. This time you will have more knowledge and tools at your disposal!

With all of the endless possibilities, the power of choice, and your purest potential, you can see how important it is to have a guide. The trek can be a bit nerve-racking and may feel overwhelming. As you fold in ADVENTURE and head down a new path in your Zone, you'll learn and create more opportunities from which to teach and master. The direction is your choice. At the end of the day, let go of the need to master and ENJOY the journey along with its many magnificent surprises.

We Learn

As small children, we were like sponges soaking up everything we could sense. Think about the many fascinating things you learned as a kid and how fun it was. You were curious and intrigued and often asked why things were the way they were. You used your imagination and maybe even played with all sorts of toys. You learned about shapes, colors, numbers, nature, mechanics, etc. Not only was it fun to learn, but you were also able to use the lessons over and over. You genuinely wanted to understand the big world around you, how stuff worked, and how to interact with everything in your surroundings. Back then, you experienced so many ADVENTURES

#32 daddy – as children, this is what we may see. They are impressionable, so offer them the best picture of yourself that you can.

and welcomed them without fear of failure. As we grew older, our learning focus shifted. Instead of absorbing knowledge to ENJOY new experiences, the emphasis of our learning efforts leaned more toward managing doubt and fear. These feelings increased as we dealt with the pain connected to failure, uncertainty, survival and competition.

Over time, many of us slow our desire to investigate new things while others start thinking they're too old to learn something new. Instead of taking on new ADVENTURES, we try to prove what we already know and, sadly, stunt our growth. As a result, we can become bored, scattered, or a bit snobbish and get stuck in our old ways. Think about it. Children act out when they're bored and their minds aren't stimulated. Teenagers like to think they know it all while almost everything and everyone around them are labeled stupid. And adults who stay in their same unchallenging jobs for years never seem to get that promotion or advancement. Although each behavior has its underlying causes, the point is that our appetite for learning fades. This decrease does not mean we stop learning. Life has a way of handing us many lessons to constantly encourage it. Nevertheless, when you stop developing yourself, you forfeit your innate ability to effectively design and direct your life.

Up to this point in your life, you've learned so much that you probably don't even realize it. Learning is unavoidable and ongoing, and most of us experience great joy when we learn something new. How cool was it when you tied your shoes, rode a bike, or kicked a ball for the first time? You perhaps even created your own way of doing it. Later on, you learned how to drive a car, take care of yourself, and earn a living. After a while, through repetition, these activities became second nature. You did them automatically while thinking about other things going on in your life.

When we think we are experts and know everything there is to know, we stop intentionally developing ourselves. It's good to be confident in what you know, but rest assured, there's always someone out there that knows more than you do. Consider being around these people as they will help you stretch your way of thinking. The knowledge you learn is powerful, but only if you can apply it and are open to other perspectives and facts. As you continue to learn, you'll grow a baseline of expertise, and through repetition, enhance your intuition in each area. The greater your intuition and desire to learn, the quicker and easier you will make choices that open doors to more ADVENTURES and create surprising results in your *Zone of Potential.*

We Create

Many of us ignore our own creative abilities. You, as a creator, have a primary purpose: to make order out of chaos that brings you value and joy while in the service of others. Although that might sound rational, the chaotic nature of our world can leave us unclear in what we are supposed to create and who we are supposed to serve. This lack of clarity can leave you feeling lost as you meander through life, but fear not. The main reason you wander may be that you haven't paid attention to what inspires and motivates you. It is only when you pause and reflect on what you've been doing that you start to see your creations and the value they bring. That's when you begin to feel a sense of purpose, mission, and meaning.

#27 psyche – our minds can be led astray by external seductive influences. Ensure your thoughts and feelings are aligned with your values and actions so you do not head down an undesirable path.

What about times when you bring value to others but still don't ENJOY life yourself? You may be too focused on meeting others' expectations. Although such selfless actions certainly are opportunities to learn and create, the fulfillment is a one-way trip if they do not bring you joy in the process. When this is the case, you may feel empty and exhausted. In the end, you'll be less inclined to share your DANCE authentically. Many of us see this in physicians and surgeons with poor bedside manners. As creators, you can choose which of your unique talents to use on your own terms and find new ways of using them so you, too, can ENJOY expressing yourself. When you truly ENJOY what you do, your service to others can be power-packed.

Law of Dharmic Direction - A guiding principle and your obligation to serve yourself and the world. This inner direction guides you to carry out your purpose and resolve your conflicts.

Above all, learning and creating are continuous and keys to every ADVENTURE. They are even more impactful when done deliberately. When you learn through set goals, you will be more focused, intentional, and RESILIENT in your creations. What you produce will bring about a sense of pride and a desire to showcase or demonstrate it to others. It is natural to do so and usually guides us in our Zone to teach.

We Teach

We love to show others what we know. It empowers us, gives us a chance to relive the feeling of our creation, and enables connections with others. This is especially true when we share what we love. Welcome this concept and you'll begin to notice that you are naturally a teacher. In fact, the vast majority of teaching occurs outside of the classroom. Teaching is where you bring your creations into the world and allow them to be experienced by others. Each time you reveal what you know, demonstrate something you can do, or provide instruction on instruments or tools, you not only offer your creation, but a chance for others to learn. By seizing these opportunities, you spread a wealth of knowledge generated during your ADVENTURE so others can also create their own.

While teaching others, make it a point to do so with understanding, flexibility, patience, and kindness. When you EMBRACE your roles as teachers and guides, keep in mind that people's challenges are unique. Everybody learns at their own pace and wants to create their own ADVENTURES. As such, each individual will choose to extract what they wish from our teachings and leave behind what does not work for them.

Life is a never-ending lesson. It is time you recognize the true teacher in yourself and the benefits of sharing your creations with others. Along the way, you will have opportunities to also learn from them and deepen your knowledge and understanding of your own journey. Through greater awareness and many ADVENTURES, you will truly begin to master your life.

We Master

Over the course of our lives, we've mastered a variety of things. You know what you have mastered because you can replicate them with ease and simplicity. You are so good at them that you have the confidence and resourcefulness to stay the course even as issues or challenges arise. What you've mastered is such an integral part of your life that you don't have to be reminded to do them. What separates mastery from habitual behaviors is your ability to remain poised when offered feedback and open to insightful responses. You have a sense of flexibility and can modify your actions on the fly to meet your purest potential.

Whatever pathway you take, striving to reach mastery comes with its challenges. At first, you might be uncomfortable or unwilling to accept feedback. Sometimes we get caught up trying to have all the answers and be right about every detail. You also may become complacent about learning and soon fall behind. A lack of progress can lead to stagnation and eventually leave you feeling irrelevant if no longer valued. As masters, we know the importance of keeping up with advancements in knowledge, skills, and technology. To continue achieving mastery in each area of your life, you must be willing to deepen your learning, open your mind to different perspectives, and engage in new ADVENTURES.

A difficulty we may experience while in mastery is when one of our ADVENTURES comes to an end, especially if we have been at it for many years. If it no longer suits your desires, matches your physical abilities, or flows freely, you may have shifted focus or met your purest potential for that ADVENTURE. Examples include former star athletes, military veterans, and retiring business tycoons. The problem encountered here is the struggle to let go of an identity still wrapped in the previous role. If a new ADVENTURE is not envisioned, they may experience an identity crisis that has the potential to lead to severe depression or harmful pleasure-seeking addictions. As a true master of your life, you have the ability to recognize the natural tendency for specific ADVENTURES to come to an end. You realize it is time to pass the torch, define a new identity, and move on to master other ADVENTURES in your Zone.

Above all ADVENTURES, is mastery of self. We master thoughts and feelings and bring them into our everyday VENTURES. The reasons we typically react or respond to certain situations is very hard to explain in the moment; we just do them. We've practiced these thoughts, feelings, and actions so often that we are

Seek self-mastery. The greatest achievement of mastery above all in life, is mastery of yourself - your actions, thoughts, and feelings. It'll last you a lifetime!

masters of them. For instance, you may always seem to be happy or sad. You learned, created, and taught others through your actions that these emotions were for you because at some point in your past they worked for you. As you ponder the ideas of your own self-mastery, consider if they are still working for you. If they are, continue developing them. If they're not, it may be worth exploring new learnings and creations that guide you toward a more rewarding and ENJOYABLE path.

ADVENTURE Barriers

As we navigate our *Zone of Potential*, we may become overwhelmed with options. Without a clear vision of what you want in your life, you can become fearful, confused, and frustrated. We have so many possibilities and yet so many excuses to stay right where we are. As you read the barriers below, pay attention to the ones you feel are holding you back. Once you identify them, you have the opportunity to learn from them and let go to grow. You are supposed to experience everything that shows up in your world. Don't fight it; learn from it! Life has a lot to offer – make the most of every moment!

When you don't know what you want, you may wander from one thing to the next. When this happens, you may become disoriented and float along with everyone else's actions or desires. It's like you can't seem to get grounded and gain traction. *Adrift.*

What happens then? You look everywhere for that perfect ADVENTURE and get nowhere. You wonder what happened and how you lost valuable time, energy, and above all, yourself. *Lost.*

There are also times when you may know what you want but you're afraid to stand out because your ADVENTURE is out of the norm. You may not want to be laughed at, pointed out, or judged. This could be embarrassing, so you don't bring your unique self forward. *Hide.*

Or, maybe you think you should wait for others to help you decide or go first. For some of us, untrekked territory can be rather frightening. Your decision to wait for others can cause you to desire more intensely, yet still you wait and miss out on new ADVENTURES. *Freeze.*

Let's say you do pick a new ADVENTURE and VENTURE in but you keep repeating the same actions and make the same decisions that keep you in the same place and get the same results. These old habits, rituals, and addictive behaviors can be masked by your desire to be efficient. What they really do is keep you comfortably right where you are. ***Stuck***.

Some people prefer or are used to being told where to go, what to do, and when to do it. Maybe you learned that you should just go with the flow and allow others to decide for you through their advice or demands. Everybody seems to know what's best for you, right? Maybe. Even kids don't like to be told what to do, yet as adults we often still do as we are told. This is when you permit others to lay out your journey rather than define and pursue your own ADVENTURES. You may feel as if you've surrendered your personal power of choice. ***Conform***.

But then, what if you do VENTURE and commit to an idea? You may end up on an ADVENTURE you didn't really want in the first place. Maybe you were thinking it could stretch your abilities, offer you new lessons, and help you determine a different path. On the other hand, it could suck you in, cause you to hyper-focus, and put all of your time and attention into an ADVENTURE that ends up being unfulfilling. This is where you fall into a comfort zone, especially as you receive accolades for your efforts. It's scary getting out of our comfort zone. If you don't challenge yourself, you may very well miss the opportunity to EMBRACE your greatest ADVENTURE yet. ***Trapped***.

And finally, after you stay in your ADVENTURE long enough, something may happen that compels you to make a change. This is the change you knew you should have made long ago. It's when you get sucked in so deep that the pain of getting out of it doesn't feel worth the effort. Yet, you also know you need to choose something different or circumstances will only lead to more pain. In our ***Zone of Potential***, the concept is coined as **'Transformation before *Devastation'*.**

When you allow these barriers to rule your life, opportunities will pass you by. Now is the time to transform your way of living so you don't devastate your life and, instead, start creating ADVENTURES that bring you lasting value and results you ENJOY. With the following ADVENTURE guiding principles you can become consciously aware of your actions and making intentional choices to navigate your world more smoothly and confidently. Who knows? Your next ADVENTURE may be your best yet!

The ADVENTURE Guide

A – AWAKEN to who you are, what is important to you, and how you express yourself.

D – DANCE to your strengths which come to you easily or energize you to dig deeper.

V – VENTURE with an intentional, purposeful, methodical approach.

E – EMBRACE where you are now as the perfect starting point to create your future.

N – NURTURE yourself and tend to valuable relationships with people, things, and events.

T – THANK and forgive yourself and others for your life experiences, even the ones yet to come.

U – UPLIFT yourself and everything in your environment for a more favorable approach.

R – RESILIENT in knowing that you have the ability to persevere and overcome obstacles.

E – ENJOY a life filled with happiness, love, joy, and peace through laughter, celebrations, and the magic each ADVENTURE brings.

We've all been given gifts and life lessons that have led us to where we are today. Our lives are supposed to be sprinkled with obstacles, puzzles, and mysteries that we can have fun overcoming, putting together, and figuring out. What you decide to do from this point on can be fascinating, one ADVENTURE at a time. In your *Zone of Potential*, you can experience anything you wish and limitless possibilities await. What you do while you are there is entirely up to you.

As you begin to use the ADVENTURE guide, you may feel somewhat overwhelmed, like there's too much to learn and apply. With that in mind, this guide breaks down the process into each letter of
A-D-V-E-N-T-U-R-E
so you can navigate your *Zone of Potential* in steps, stages, or as a whole in and of itself.

Grab a cup of your favorite beverage and join me in unfolding the excitement of your life as the greatest ADVENTURE you'll ever experience in your *Zone of Potential!*

AWAKEN

*O*ur physical lives on Earth are far too short to settle for anything less than something meaningful and fulfilling. We see people doing amazing things all of the time and wonder how that can be us. Instead of trying new things, many of us go through our lives on a mundane track to our own deathbeds. The excitement we endure ends up being the frustrations we encounter. Time and time again, we repeat the same activities, day after day, rarely making or taking advantage of opportunities to truly live fully.

When we know who we are, what we really want, and how we must be to get it, we'll become more aware of what has kept us stuck. Awareness is the first step to help you move past what isn't working for you. If you are willing to change your beliefs and what you do, you may just uncover your purpose, meaning, and unique proposition to the world. You have the power to design your life any way you want. When you AWAKEN to that idea, you'll begin to see life as a series of amazing ADVENTURES all created by you and for you.

In order to benefit from the material throughout this book, you may want to periodically reflect back on this chapter. It contains nuggets of information that fold into your entire way of living. Each chapter is about aligning with who you are, what's valuable to you, and what you're willing to do. All of your discoveries and choices from here will affect your entire life. Happy reading!

I Am

Have you ever wondered who you really are or are supposed to be? Many know exactly why they're here while others spend their lifetimes searching for their calling. Whatever the case may be, we adopt certain lifestyles, roles, and jobs based on our own decisions and what others want for us or expect of us. To validate and feel true to these characteristics, we describe

#1 good morning, little one – as you AWAKEN to who you are, you may begin to remember that you are on a quest to evolve your beautiful soul.

ourselves and sculpt our personalities accordingly. As time passes, we continue to accept and live out these self-created identities that bring us fulfilling lives or lead us to feel empty, lost, and hopeless. If it's the latter you experience and you yearn for something different, just know that you're not alone in this quest. Many of us don't realize that we are here to live peaceful, ENJOYABLE, loving lives. We can only do so if we look beyond our self-made identities, learn to appreciate who we really are, and follow our true life's purpose.

Humans Facing Cause and Effect

We all possess the ability to theorize, create, and communicate our conceptual ideas through words and actions. It's one of the wonderful aspect about ourselves that sets us apart from other animals. As intelligent human beings, we find ways to get what we want through preparation, support, and action. This use of our intellect is how we individually create the reality of what we see, hear, and feel in our lives today.

Along with our intelligent thoughts, we are also our own dharma and karma. Although there's no single word for dharma in the English language, it essentially stands for an aim in life with connected behaviors used to design our lives. It's basically our mission or purpose where we use our acquired knowledge and abilities mixed with our genius to gift creations into the world.

When we are not guided by our dharma, we are reacting to the effects of karma. Our karma is what we receive as a result of our behavior. Every action will receive a reaction. This is true in both positive or negative circumstances. We continuously experience bouts of karma as we make decisions. If you're living primarily through the effects of karma and not aware of your dharma, you will encounter barriers in discovering your purpose and learning your life's lessons. That said, your dharma and karma heavily influence who you have become and how you choose to act.

Law of Karma – You decide what you need to learn for your life along with who and what will help you master those lessons.

Although past actions and current beliefs offer us good indications of who we think and feel we are, they were guided by what was and is in our environment. Your surroundings offer you clues to the roles you've been playing, how you've been operating, and who you've chosen as friends and associates. Ultimately, we have become the person we chose to be based on what we decided for ourselves.

We all come from different backgrounds, grow up with different view-points, and experience things in our own special ways. It doesn't matter if we were raised with the same family, lived in the same household, or had similar experiences. Each one of us takes from our experiences and creates who we want to be. My large family of seven children offers a great example of this.

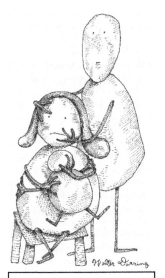

I didn't realize, until I started asking questions, how vastly different each one of my brothers and sisters experienced their upbringing. Although we lived in the same house with the same people and experienced many of the same events, each of us processed what we saw and heard in our own way. By using of this information, we developed our unique personalities to deal with life's challenges.

#21 the family – the depth of our connections, acceptance of our differences, and willingness to support one another define what we consider to be family.

Curious, I asked my sisters about how they felt as children and what they wanted growing up. I was greatly surprised and quite amused by our differences. For example, as the sixth child of seven and the youngest girl, I conformed to the family and went with the flow of what everyone else wanted. This generated a feeling of being trapped and shaped my desire for spontaneity. My sisters, on the other hand, wanted more support, structure, and safety. As such, we each created roles and shaped our environments to experience our ideas of freedom, care, order, and security to suit our wants.

Although we wanted other things, this illustrates our uniqueness in who we are and how we've come to be. This profound realization has brought me to a place of deeper love and respect for all of my sisters and brothers. I know I will never fully understand all of our nuances, but I have a better appreciation of our unique qualities as beautiful human beings. We all want a sense of achievement, closeness, security, freedom, structure, excitement, and connection. It's the degree in which each of us seeks them that drives us and makes us stand out.

All of our situations are unique. Keep an open mind and be receptive to whatever thoughts show up in your differences. At the same time, be careful when projecting judgments. It's your duty to recognize who you really are and what you want to be so you can feel authentic, valued, and purposeful. As you discover what you did and wanted as a child, you will start to reveal who you've been telling yourself you are. With that awareness, you can then decide if it is truly what you want or if you want to be something different.

> *Study who you have been. What you discover will empower you to move in the direction of who you want to be. Just remember, this knowledge is power, but only if you use it.*

As aspiring masters of our world, we each have a unique purpose. With the use of your intellect, experiences, and surroundings, you have been creating a life that brings out your most authentic self. We are all uniquely beautiful with our individual values, beliefs, and attitudes on a mission to master our lives and help others do the same. As you read on, you may discover that your purest authenticity is driven by our deepest values. When you AWAKEN to who "I am", you can harmonize with your values and make intentional choices for a more purposeful ADVENTURE and life.

I Value

Living our lives meaningfully and purposefully starts with our values. Many of us do not realize how much our values play into our decisions. You have used them to create who you are, guide what you do, and select what you bring into your world. They are the catalysts that drive your actions with a main intent to either honor them or protect them. This comes naturally to all of us.

Up to this point in your life, your values have helped you experience amazing ADVENTURES. You can see the results of them all around you in how you live your life today. Although your deep-seated values, also known as core values, don't normally change drastically, the ones you can see change as aspects of your life change. For instance, you may not be readily aware of deep-seated values that enticed you to choose your friends. Since your parents or guardians guided you in developing your values, you will very likely discover the same ones in your friends that you experienced with your guardians. Some examples of deeper values not physically noticeable that you look for in friends may include loyalty, freedom, enthusiasm, honesty, and integrity, among many others. Observable values that you can identify quickly, on the other hand, might be beauty, money, connections, intellect, etc. As you hang out together, you'll know your friendship is an ideal choice for you when these values align and you complement one another. In the same respect, people will fall away as each of you experience shifts or clarity in your values.

Your values extend beyond your relationships with people. They are also the primary factors you use to determine what items you want to bring into your life and experience. We often feel a passion for having or doing something, yet we cannot seem to put our finger on why. When this happens, you are dealing with a deep-seated value. These obscure values are so vague that they are mysterious and challenge our ability to identify and describe them. All we know is that we have a strong urge to bring those specific people, things, or experiences into our lives.

> *Live your values. If you aren't honoring your values, you may be living someone else's. If your values aren't serving you well, shift them so they do.*

We also may not be aware of why we respond with enthusiasm or defend ourselves when questioned. These are good indicators that can reveal or lead to discovering your core values. When you AWAKEN to your values, you will notice your easier and faster decisions are based on your values. You will be more comfortable letting go of things and saying no to events that don't allow you to bring out your best. You will find yourself inspired, focused, and happier because of it. They, in and of themselves, are a huge factor necessary to make life your favorite ADVENTURE.

What We Love and Believe

While we all value many of the same things, the way we live with those things is unique to each one of us. We developed our core values pre-adulthood. They are what we love in life that we constantly seek to include in our experiences. If you look around, you will find things and people from your past that gave you great joy and many that you still ENJOY. Examples of things that reflect value are the souvenirs, tools, relics, and photos you collected over time. You can determine the value of people in your life by who you call or visit, how often you make contact, and the effort you put forth to see them. The idea here is not about the actual things or people, but more so about the clues they leave to help you identify your deep values. You will see evidence everywhere and in everything you have and do. These clues divulge your truths about who you have been and how you express yourself today through what you value.

Along with their vagueness, another challenge we share in detecting our core values is that we bury them under differing beliefs. Sometimes this can confuse us. For instance, you and your intimate partner may value fun in your relationships. Fun is very vague and carries different meanings. At first, you both may have agreed to what you considered fun. As time goes on, conditions change. What you believed was fun in your earlier years together may no longer be fun for one or both of you today. That does not mean you don't value fun anymore. It's that your belief about what it means to have fun is simply something different from what it was in the past. This contradiction causes a lot of disagreements in couples when one person changes the meaning of their values through new beliefs while the other does not.

> ⚡ *Adjust your beliefs to honor your values. Your beliefs are what you think about to determine how you bring your values into the world. Your values are how you think about yourself.*

So how can we tell the difference between a value and a belief? One way is to examine the flexibility in the situation. If whatever you want is non-negotiable, you can be pretty sure it is a value. On the other hand, if you could go either way or easily sway your opinion or decision, it is very likely a belief. For example, most of us value love in our intimate relationships. Typically, that's why we have them, to give and receive the love we desire. As part of expressing love, you may believe that gift exchanges are how you know you're receiving it. Does that mean if you don't receive gifts that the person doesn't love you? Not really. It may be something you prefer, and if you think about it, the person very likely still loves you. They may just believe that love is expressed in other manners than yours.

Going back to the example of fun mentioned above, let's imagine you both see fun as amusing, playful, and lighthearted activities. Both of you were able to honor that in each other when you were attending parties, going to concerts, bar hopping, and doing other empty-nest activities. Once you decide to bring children into the mix or some other life-changing event happens, your beliefs about parties, concerts, and bars may not fit well with the new family dynamics or belief about what is fun for you. Your value about having fun is still there, but your beliefs on how to go about it evolved to consider your new values and priorities. You may still see these activities as fun, but they are now negotiable and easily pushed aside. Frustration in the relationship and life comes into play when one or both persons don't change their beliefs to fit a new lifestyle. If you do not create new, shared ideas about what fun can be, you will exclude other valuable parts of your life and struggle to integrate your old and new beliefs. It may feel as if you're not growing as a couple. Either one of you may become more protective of the new or old beliefs, especially when directly challenged. When this happens, you can be sure to expect an influx of conflict and disagreements in your future.

> *Alter your beliefs to shape your life. You do not need a tight grip on them, just a good understanding of how they affect your values.*

Law of Belief – You can have everything you want if you give up believing you can't have it. This law is true as long as it does not conflict with someone else's belief.

Another way to determine your values is through your attitudes that directly tie to your beliefs. It's easy to recognize your attitude as it is the first trigger you encounter when faced with a thought or decision. It is how you immediately react to certain things, people, and events that you like or dislike. Similar to beliefs, it comes from your usual way of thinking and feeling. It is easy to detect as you can feel it in your body, and others can normally pick up on it in your physical reactions and expressions.

Let's again expand on the example about fun. When you discuss with your partner how life's priorities have changed and the need to change behaviors, you may encounter a certain reaction. Maybe you experience red faces, raised voices, and hand gestures. On the flip side, you may encounter agreement through thoughtful discussions and idea exchanges, head nodding, and relaxed body postures. All of these are signs of attitudes attached to beliefs about the value of fun along with any other values that may be prompted.

Pay attention to feelings in your heart, head, and belly. They offer clues to your attitude of whether your beliefs are moving toward pleasure or away from pain associated with your values.

Attitudes are neither good nor bad in and of themselves. They're simply expressions of beliefs tied to values. Because you can typically notice them rather quickly, you'll find them much easier to change than your beliefs and values. They are merely behaviors that, like a habit, can be embraced or instantly dropped when you resolve the challenge of the belief. The choice is yours.

As you trace your attitudes through your beliefs to your values, you will better understand what inspires you to take action. If you ignore your attitudes, you may continue to do things you know you shouldn't or drag your feet on those things you know you should. You will find your life easier to navigate when you support your values with helpful updated beliefs and attitudes. As an added benefit, this renewed perspective may inspire you to make even greater changes in your life.

 Law of Attitude - Our individual responses are all different and move us toward events to intensify or ease them.

I Do

Many of us are asleep to what we do day in and day out. We wake up the same way at the same time, use the same restroom, eat the same breakfast, take the same shower, put on the same clothes, and go the same route to the same place of work. We deal with the same people in the same way at home and at work.

We use the same tools, equipment, and furniture the same way. Our chairs sink in the same place our butts have been. Our books sit unused, collecting dust. Our exercise equipment pose as second laundry baskets and clothes racks. We go about our days without fully paying attention and unconsciously neglect what once was valuable. Despite all of this, we deliberately brought and kept people and items in our world for a purpose. Even though we may not feel inspired or motivated to make them an active part of our daily living, we once did.

We not only neglect people and things, we also buzz around them as if they're sitting still. We dote over them, talk over them, and walk over them. Rarely do we pause to question the impact our busy-ness leaves on what is important to us. Instead, we continue our busy moments in an effort to hide some pain we have yet to face or satisfy some egotistic need. Alas, we become so busy doing, that we miss out on the value and beauty of our surroundings and everyone in it. John Bogle, author of Enough, says, "Each of us must decide for ourselves how much to focus on things, and indeed what things to focus on…each of us can profit by some moments of quiet introspection about whether our lives are driven far too much by the accumulation of things, and not nearly enough by the exercise of bold commitment to our family, to our work, to a worthy cause, to our society, and to our world." Quite frankly, just because you are busy does not mean you are tending to what is most important to you. If you continue, one day you may wake up with nothing, all alone, and lonely.

> Be aware of what you're doing and why. Your actions say more about you than any words can ever describe. What life deals you is real. What you do with it is the real deal.

If you are not living by and honoring your highest values, you will not feel inspired to do what you say you will. If you don't have an incentive to do certain things, you will be less motivated to do them. Finally, if your motivation doesn't harmonize with your inspiration, you will eventually become frustrated and struggle to reach your purest potential.

Inspired Action is an Internal Pull

Inspired activities make your heart sing. They are events you love doing, can't get enough of, or can't stop thinking about doing again. We act with inspiration when we do things that feel natural, bring us lasting joy, and satisfy our passions. They align directly with your values, and when you do not experience them in some way, you may feel empty, unfulfilled, or incomplete.

When your actions do not align with your values, you may feel inauthentic, forced, and discontent. It's like you're doing what others want you to do.

If you knew what you truly valued right now, you would find it easier to give up trivial activities and do more of what makes you feel alive. This feeling lets you know you're living inspired. The thing is, most of the time it doesn't always just come to you. Merely watching people do miraculous things may inspire you, but that doesn't mean you will do them. You have to know that driving feeling and take steps to move yourself in that direction. That might be easier said than done, but your past can help you identify it. You will see indications of your valued activities in your overused, worn-out things, what you regularly replace, and what you cherish or keep in mint condition.

A Marine Colonel who presided over my retirement from the Marine Corps is a testament to inspired action. Frank dedicated over 37 years of active duty in the Corps, defending our nation, leading troops, motivating brothers in arms, and carrying out orders, all with a love for Frank Sinatra tunes in his soul. He was influenced by music from the 40's, 50's, and 60's from many musicians of that era and sang all of his life. Although he loved the Corps just as much, he knew when he retired from serving his nation that his new career as a Frank Sinatra tribute singer and entertainer had to be next. As a self-taught entertainer, Frank launched his dream and has been performing *Frank Sings Frank* magical, musical acts for over a decade on the US East Coast and on cruise ships. During his performances, he inspires every person in the crowd to participate by dancing, tapping, and clapping to the music. Sometimes they even get a chance to sing with him. Frank loves what he does and capitalizes on every opportunity to getting behind the mike and passionately singing his heart out.

Motivated Action is an External Push

We also do things when we are motivated by external factors. These are the incentive-based carrot or stick led actions. When we engage in motivational activities, we may fulfill a need of safety, security, or recognition. Although motivation also aligns with your values, they are often tied more closely to your beliefs and attitudes. We are enticed by things or people that we believe will offer us pleasure or help us avoid pain. Unfortunately, many of us don't become motivated to act until faced with the fear of missing out, loss, or negative feedback about something

Do what you love for no other reason than you love to do it! When you're inspired to do what you love, you believe in yourself and want to reach further. Motivation, on the other hand, has a tendency to end without lasting commitment.

important to us. Imagine harnessing what inspires you and incentivizing it. That is how highly successful businesses and dream jobs come to life.

How We Show Up

The way we present ourselves speaks volumes to who we are and how we think. Most of the time, we are not even aware of the image we portray. The way we show up projects through our bodies, energy, emotions, and, of course, language. People can pick up on your confidence, shyness, and openness, among other traits, simply by recognizing your posture and body position. Through your gestures, you continuously act out who you think and feel you are. For instance, a simple body, hand, or mouth gesture can indicate many of our beliefs and attitudes. The way you sit, stand, and walk can reveal your personality. We use our hands to emphasize communications and orchestrate emotions through waving, pounding, clapping, putting certain fingers up, etc.

The information you receive directly from others reflects how they see you and can be quite revealing. People give us such great insights through their lens of verbal descriptions, physical responses, and emotional reactions. Although we do not have to believe everything people say about us, the way they respond to us offers clues about our behavior, emotions, thoughts, and energy. By paying attention to others' verbal and nonverbal reactions, we can determine how similar we think our behaviors are to what they see.

> *Ask others to describe how they see you. Many of us may be shocked to hear what others see in us. Receive it without judgment regardless.*

People are not the only feedback sources you can use. Your body also tells you how you are showing up. When you tremble, scrunch your eyebrows, or sulk, you can easily tell that you are nervous, angry, or sad. Your body can also tell you whether your thoughts are empowering or discouraging by the physical strength you display in certain situations. Your view of the world is expressed in your body posture, actions, and words that communicate with you through symptoms. These symptoms are messages telling you when you are on track or you have exceeded your physical, mental, or emotional tolerance. Your goal for a fulfilling life is to experience healthy symptoms associated with love, joy, and peace. In order to treat your unhealthy symptoms, you can begin by altering how you think, feel, and act.

How you carry yourself speaks volumes to who you believe you are. Unless you consider how others see or hear you, you will not have a fair appreciation of who you are being. People will never fully understand or recognize what and why you do things, but they can give you valuable perspectives as to what they are experiencing with you. This information can be most insightful when you are following a routine and not paying attention. People often see what we don't, including how we are with our possessions and friends. It all speaks volumes about who we are, what's important to us, and how we usually present ourselves. If we ignore others' feedback, we may create barriers in becoming our best selves. Over time, this might be baffling as we watch these obstacles grow more extensive than we hoped or intended.

I Will

We all have an amazing amount of personal power we can access. Our personal power is what we use to decide what we want and what we are

#53 tree gods – with an optimal environment trees and plants can grow powerfully right where they are. People must find their optimal environment to nourish their growth and become the masters of their lives.

willing to do to get it. It offers us opportunities to use our imagination, choose what we want, and bring it to life. This ability goes beyond any other species' capabilities on this earth. Animals are relatively comfortable with their environment because they quickly learn to conform and adapt. Plants cannot grow everywhere. Trees and shrubs cannot uproot themselves and move south for the winter. While plants and animals must adapt, humans have the ability to go, do, and be as we please. Above all, we have the power of free will to think, feel, and imagine anything our hearts desire.

As a human, you are empowered and free to live the life of your dreams. The funny thing is, instead of intentionally making decisions to obtain our dreams, we often seem to get lost. We face so many questions and options that we become disoriented. We often think we want what others have, yet we are not willing to do what it takes to get them. We begin to believe we can't make it happen for us. The challenge might be that what we wanted wasn't necessarily consistent with what we were willing to do. It is all about intention! Just desiring something will not bring it into existence. You must intend to be, have, or do whatever it is you want. Let's face it, there are things we are willing to do and many we are not. To live life like it is your favorite ADVENTURE is to know what you want and what you are willing to do to go after it.

> *Focus on what is most important. Everything that brings lasting value and joy is worth your time and effort, no matter how big or small. If you do not invest in your values, people will overpower yours with theirs.*

Ultimately, you are responsible for creating your own happiness, discovering your joy within, and deciding what will bring you lasting value. In the same vein, others are responsible for their own happiness, joy, and value. You must be willing to make easy and hard decisions based on what is truly important to you. At the end of the day, without a will to decide and act, you will struggle with your journey. With a will, comes a way!

Law of Denial - Your refusal to handle or take responsibility will affect you until corrected.

It All Begins with Freewill

As humans, we were gifted with freewill to think, feel, and act as we desire. You can make conscious choices to change every area in your life and to create something totally different, if you so desire. That is called freewill. You can decide what you want to do for work, depth of relationships, quality of health, type of religion, size of your home, and so on. You can also choose how much time and effort you put into everything you do or have. Finally, you can choose what route you want to take to get there.

This freedom of choice can be a blessing if you know what is important to you. It can also be very stressful if you don't know what you want. When we get caught up in information and condition loops, we get stuck and find it hard to make decisions. Most of the time, these loops are driven by our own fears of getting trapped with a bad choice. Instead, we continue to research and endlessly put off our decisions. We also may end up making choices based on what others have or want us to have instead of what aligns with our own values and ENJOYMENT. This conflict of interest challenges our ability to use our willpower wisely.

When you do not tap into your willpower, you become less enthusiastic to reach your goal or appreciate small successes along the way. This lack of willpower quite often leads to indecision and procrastination. Just the thought of having to make a decision drags you down and drains you of your strength. Instead, you rationalize yourself into believing you can't do them and right out of potential exciting ADVENTURES.

It doesn't have to be like this. Freewill is such a gift, especially if you know how to use it to your greatest advantage. As you AWAKEN to the identity you want to assume and what is important to you, you will find new energy inside of you that helps you use your freewill wisely and intentionally.

> **Law of Free Will - As you flow with your freedom to choose, you minimize tension, detach from negativity, and leave karma behind.**

Can't or Won't?

Once you recognize and accept that freewill gives us an abundance of personal power, you may start to realize you also have the power to do anything within your reasoning. The word "can't" may no longer seem to fit into your vocabulary because willpower isn't about whether you can or can't. The words "I can't" denote the actual ability to do something. With very few exceptions, you can do anything for yourself or with help from people and technology. If you want something bad enough, you'll do what it takes to get it. You have to be able to imagine it, and it has to be realistic and possible.

> *Start using the words "I choose not to" versus "I can't." You will be happiest when you decide what you want. By harnessing your freewill, you can make intentional choices that align with your greatest values.*

A few examples of unrealistic scenarios include body structure, aging, and controlling others. For example, if your height is five feet and you want to be six feet tall, you'd have to go through some major surgery or strap on stilts to be a foot taller. It would be unrealistic for you to expect to actually grow that tall as it's not physically possible. The same goes for aging. Although many people can move through it gracefully, the only way to stop it is to no longer exist. That's not normally the option we would prefer. As for controlling other's behaviors, you can influence, manipulate, and physically handle people, but that doesn't necessarily mean you can control their thoughts, feelings, and actions. People aren't robots, and they too have freewill and willpower to think, feel, and do as they please.

People constantly use their freewill and perform amazing feats due to their desire to achieve them. We've all heard of people who are immobile or missing certain parts of their bodies yet still doing what they love without them. Stephen Hawking had no ability to physically move or speak, yet he became one of the world's most prominent scientists and authors. The amazing blind musician and composer, Stevie Wonder earned his first music record label before hitting his teenage years. He also wrote songs. Helen Keller was deaf and blind, yet she still wrote and lectured. These are only a few well-known examples of people who saw their disability as a part of life but not a barrier to stop them from carrying out their life's purpose. Here is one of many examples I've experienced with people doing what they love while defying their disabilities.

> *Tap into your personal power of freewill and willpower. Since you can do anything you set your mind to, use your personal power to intentionally decide what you want and your willingness to do what it takes.*

As I was walking my dog by a school one day, I glanced over at the tennis courts and noticed that one of the coaches was missing an arm. I thought it was quite fascinating and later learned his story. Despite being born without one of his arms, he loved playing tennis as a kid and was very good at it. He hadn't thought twice about it throughout his school years as he was encouraged by family and friends and won many games and awards for his skills. He never really doubted his abilities until it was time for him to decide what to do as a profession. He truly wanted to be an athletic coach but was concerned he'd never be taken seriously by others. Overcoming his doubts of anyone hiring a one-armed tennis player, he stayed true to his dream and earned his degree in exercise science anyway. Today, the administration at his local prestigious private school recognizes his contributions. His students love his teaching and coaching style and playing tennis with him. His success was due to his determination and the use of his freewill to choose his dreams and relentless willpower to pursue them. Just like this tennis player, you have the power to do what you love.

Have faith in yourself, know you can do it, and go for it.

A major showstopper many of us encounter in harnessing our willpower is through the use of the words, "I can't." Stated aloud, this phrase gives a disempowering feeling and depresses our energy. It can lead us to believe we won't succeed even before we begin. Normally the problem isn't that you can't. It's typically that you don't know how or haven't decided to fully commit. If it's something you desire bad enough and are willing to put forth the effort, you'll figure out how. Remember, the power is in your hands to choose.

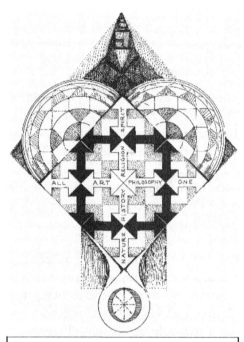

#73 the sacred heart – the complexity of the mind is wrapped in how we think and feel. By knowing what we hold dear, we simplify the complexity in our decisions.

There are many things in life that you may not be willing to do. Maybe your "I can't" is really "I won't" because you are uninterested or unwilling to do whatever it takes to achieve it. Saying "I won't" is much more empowering and decisive. It means you live by choice. If that's the case, it may be time to change your language from "I can't" to "I won't". You can do anything if you want it badly enough. By recognizing the difference between what you want and what you're willing to do to get it, you'll stop wasting your time and choose more wisely. Accepting the reality that you won't commit the effort to certain endeavors frees you to choose new goals that better suit you and your life.

Law of Mind – Join the brain and heart into oneness.

New Experiences

You have unlimited possibilities and an abundance of potential. Once you know what you're willing to do, you will realize you can create any new experience you desire. Your brain may run wild with ideas, and you may feel like you can do anything. It can be fun and exciting, but if the number of thoughts becomes overwhelming, consider your values and the roles you want to play. Remember, although you don't have to continue in the same roles, you will still feel a strong desire to honor and protect what's important to you. Therefore, ensure the roles you choose and values mesh.

As opportunities pop up for new experiences, you may not immediately envision the value they might bring. Your focus will be a key ingredient to help you recognize what's happening and seize opportunities as they arise. With clarity, you are also able to identify what to VENTURE into now and what can be done later as your life unfolds.

#39 life on earth – we all have aspirations from basic to technical. ENJOY and master your greatness!

New experiences motivate us to stretch ourselves. They offer a sense of authenticity, empowerment, and control. Many of them will inspire and encourage us to open ourselves up and prepare for more to come. This cascade effect of new experiences not only gives us feelings of happiness and confidence, it also allows us to ENJOY the unfolding of a new reality.

Law of Experience – The brain is in an endless state of growth and development. The introduction of new experiences allows us to expand our knowledge and replace outdated information.

New Reality

Every new experience brings with it a shift in our reality. You find more comfort in making wiser choices, changing your environment, forming new memories, and adjusting your language as your attitudes, beliefs, and values evolve. From a sensory point of view, you will experience different sights, sounds, textures, smells, and maybe even tastes. Your space will fill with new items, or you'll detach from old belongings. You'll hear new lingering noises and surprising comments from others. You might even feel a little more at ease about your surroundings and yourself as your perspectives change.

You also have the ability to generate new experiences by creating a new reality. To intentionally create a new reality, you visualize and plan your days with clarity and flexibility. Put forth your best effort during peak hours and on one thing at a time. Exercise your brain by using your willpower and staying disciplined. Create helpful routines, avoid distractions, and concentrate on living in the moment. The more you intentionally develop and shape your reality, the more you'll ENJOY your new experiences.

When you create your new reality, you can live fully, authentically, and bravely. You will find it easier to assume full responsibility for creating your life and living it to the best of your ability. You will likely engage in activities you want to do daily and do it with pride. You won't dwell on your past behaviors or emotions. You become intentional and actively pursue your desires. You will discover that you are ultimately in control of yourself and can flex easily with activities in your environment.

> *Open your arms, mind, and heart to experience life a little differently. With what comes in, create the reality of your dreams and ENJOY the fun and ADVENTURE your creations bring.*

Over the years, I started becoming aware of how my life had taken shape and the risks I faced. Some activities were pretty easy to understand, others not so much. One of the more questionable, but proudest, experiences I willfully VENTURED into was participating in bodybuilding competitions. At that point in time, I was having marital problems and spent most of my free time at the gym working off frustration. Although I saw plenty of people working out, it hadn't even dawned on me that any of them were training for anything other than improving their health and maybe their physical fitness.

A bodybuilder in the gym approached me and asked if I wanted to join their group and train for a contest. At first, I was hesitant due to time constraints and priorities, but after I gave it some thought, I agreed. Years later, as I pondered my decision to join the group of competitors, I became aware that bodybuilding fed into who I wanted to be, my values of fitness and fun, and what I was already doing. I have always considered myself an athlete, and this time I was invited to be included as one. Being accepted as part of the group was huge for me. I would never have intruded on them or asked them to join. I felt like I fit in, and the thought of experiencing different exercises and learning new things made my heart sing.

My initial concerns about available time and of life priorities were not nearly as difficult as I believed them to be, and the decision was really relatively easy. My reality started to change the minute after I committed. As my bodybuilding ADVENTURE unfolded, I noticed people treated me differently. They seemed more cordial and approachable. Opportunities started popping up too. I met Mr. Olympia and other celebrities, was offered special work assignments, and educated myself as a personal fitness trainer. It opened up a whole new world and reality for me that I never even considered. I will always be thankful for having the courage to say "I will" to this lifechanging ADVENTURE!

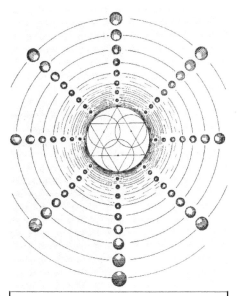

With new experiences and new reality, you will soon realize life is an ADVENTURE in and of itself and filled with wonderful surprises. It all begins with AWAKENING to who you've

#51 surprise – we may be born into a world of chaos, but as we AWAKEN, clarity and order will begin to take shape. Everything is in order; we simply need to uncover it!

created in yourself, what you've been doing, and what's important to you now. When those three aspects become clearer, you'll be more in tune with what you're willing to do to create new experiences and a new reality, ones that are more in line with the fulfilling life you deserve.

DANCE

*D*ANCE, DANCE, DANCE. Your DANCE is a finessed combination of your talents, knowledge, and skills and is more valuable than any degree, certificate, or trophy. With this magical trio we feel confident, competent, and empowered. When we are self-assured in what we are doing, know all the steps, and are in the rhythm and flow of the music, we love to express our DANCE. That is also how we feel when we use our strengths. Your DANCE is uniquely yours and is what gives you energy, power, and strength to perform like no other.

Talented You

The baseline for your DANCE starts with your talents. Although we mostly associate talents with our physical abilities, they also emerge from our mental and emotional traits. For example, people with mental talents are incredibly skilled at strategy, attention to detail, problem-solving, and anything that uses logic, reason, and understanding. To break it down further, people who excel in strategy include chess players, planners, and sports coaches. Those who have a flair for attention to detail would excel as public accountants, archeologists, and editors. These are only a few examples of those with intellectual qualities.

Examples of emotional talents include compassion, courage, and the ability to motivate others. People with compassion perform well as care providers and public servants. Those who tend to be very courageous will likely thrive in exhilarating or extreme sports, public safety, and dangerous high-altitude jobs. For our motivators, they may shine as excellent speakers, coaches, and teachers. Since these examples are based on one talent only, the integration of other natural abilities will further clarify areas where you will excel.

Given that our talents feel natural and are unique to each one of us, they are often mistaken as our DANCE. Although foundational pieces, they still require development to turn them into something you do well, comfortably, and with flow. Therefore, fortify your talents with knowledge, learn how to use them wisely, and practice. By purposely enhancing your talents with knowledge and skills, you open yourself to achieving extraordinary results. It is this intentional development and usage of talents that help you EMBRACE your personal DANCE and leave a lasting impression on the world.

Your challenge in recognizing your DANCE may be if you continue to hold onto the idea that talents are physical. Acknowledge, and do not discount, that you possess talent beyond your physical capabilities, or you will shortchange opportunities to do what comes so naturally for you. If you don't recognize them, these invisible talents can also become a hinderance if overused. Balance, perspective, and awareness are keys to employing your talents effectively and gaining the results you desire. Sharpen these natural abilities so you can bring out the best of yourself consistently. With the confidence, poise, and finesse you develop in your DANCE, you become magnanimous and unstoppable!

We all have different talents and varying degrees to which we are aware of, use, and develop them. You may be using your talents every chance you get, regardless of how you feel about the feedback. You also may apply them loosely in different areas of your life at your convenience. The bottom line is you develop and use your talents perfectly the way you know how to satisfy your individual needs. The more you enhance them with knowledge and skills, the more fully you will be able to use them throughout all areas in your life.

> ✒ *Master using your talents. They are unique to you and nobody can take them away from you.*

Law of Restriction – *You only create that which comes from your current individual understanding, nothing higher. Work from the inside out, not the outside in, in order to change your world.*

Knowledge

We never stop learning, and there's so much we individually have yet to discover! Regardless of whether we know a lot about a few things or a little about many things, the opportunity to deepen our understanding is limitless. As you increase your knowledge, keep in mind that it is only valuable if you use it wisely and often. Indeed, if you do not, you may struggle to retain and reuse what you've learned.

What you know up to this point didn't just come from the schoolhouse. It all comes from various places and primarily from three main information sources; data, practice, and intuition. And the information you acquire helps shape your book smarts (externally driven), street smarts (internally chosen), and worldly smarts (universally accessible). Knowledge is created by taking in bits of data, processing it through what you perceive, and forming a reasoned explanation for it. That information then becomes what you understand and use at that moment. And, with this collective information, you intellectually strengthen your intuitive capabilities to make quicker, more fitting decisions.

Our data-driven information is primarily static. Marcus Buckingham and Donald O. Clifton, in their book, *Now, Discover Your Strengths*, call this factual knowledge. You gain this information from reading material, observing activities in your environment, exploring things, and listening to what is going on in the world. Examples include books, magazines, television, radio, casual conversations, lectures, and the list goes on.

As posed by Buckingham and Clifton, practiced or experiential information is the knowledge we gain from doing. We acquire it through physical behaviors, such as tying our shoes, riding our bikes, or assembling things. They are often supported by data-driven knowledge. Because we use more of our senses, we gain a deeper understanding of them through the actual experience. For instance, you can read about riding a bike all day long, but you will never know how it really works until you actually swing a leg over the seat and ride it.

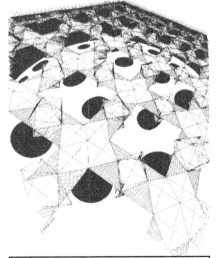

And then there is intuitive information, what some people like to call 'knowing.' This is what we just know and have difficulty describing because it is part of our inner core. Our intuitive information comes from the language of the heart and is often derived from patterns we learned through our practiced-derived knowledge. In his book *The Power of Intuition*, Gary Klein defines intuition as a way we translate our experiences into judgments and decisions. He says that when we use

#47 einstein – "The intuitive mind is a sacred gift and the rational mind is a faithful servant." Albert Einstein

cues and patterns from situations, we quickly and instinctively run them through various scenarios of response actions to decide how to react. Our intuitive information can seem mysterious, but for some reason, we know to trust in our feeling of knowing. We tend to use our intuition more than we know, but many of us just do not pay much attention to it and write it off as good luck or coincidence and bad luck or Murphy's law. When we begin to use our intuition, we will find it is a gift guided by our intentional thoughts of what we want. The key is to recognize and trust it, unlike I did before one of my stock purchases went belly-up!

Before the market crash in 2008, I decided to try my hand in individual stock investments. I had learned about stocks and investing in college and read many books from prominent authors about how to invest. With a sense of responsibility and enough knowledge to feel courageous, I gave it a whirl. As stocks sank to record lows, I purchased common stock in a major department store that I knew well and shopped frequently. I thought the brand-name legacy store would be an eternal iconic legend and was a relatively safe investment. For years, I watched it hit new highs and sometimes go rather low. I bought more shares at the lows and sat on them at the highs. I had faith in the store and certainly did not consider the possibility of it going out of business. When news article after news article discussed threats of potential bankruptcy, I ignored my intuition to sell and justified my actions with the idea that news outlets make a lot of noise to influence people. It was a costly lesson when the stock went to zero, but it also taught be a lot about the risks in financial investing and the need to trust my intuition. Sometimes when we think we have it all figured out, life has a tendency to challenge our notions and hand us other opportunities to learn. It's the universe's way of kicking us out of our comfort zones and encouraging growth. That's exactly what I learned from my mistake.

Our level of knowledge will continue to change as we shift our focus from one ADVENTURE to another. As life goes on, many of us will find our desire to keep learning slows down. This happens because you begin to recognize many of the same situations, relearn the same lessons, and lean on more habits and routines. Experience in itself is not all a bad thing because it also allows you to sharpen your intuition. In the same breath, be careful not to shortchange yourself by believing you no longer need to learn

> ⚡ *Realize that you do not know everything, will never know everything, and it is okay not to know everything. Thinking we know everything is an illusion of the ego, stunts our growth, and endangers our progress.*

anymore. Learning is one of the many reasons new challenges are so exciting, and experiences make it fun through renewed energy, new direction, and opportunities to create.

As you increase your knowledge, you open a gateway to greater breadth and depth of intuitively knowing when and where to apply it. This strengthens our talents, increases our self-confidence, and creates exciting opportunities. It is up to each one of us to use our knowledge intentionally and be inquisitive to learn more as we apply it. When we boost our knowledge with skills to express our talent, we will sharpen our DANCE and do it with consistency.

#62 allegory of the ego – although this drawing can seem quite gruesome and dark, it is a good depiction of what happens when we let our egos rule our worlds. At the end of the day, you'll continue to find in others and attract that which you want or do not want in yourself.

Skills

Each one of us has skills and use them every day in everything we do. Our skills are structured processes that, when applied, help us get things done. They feed into our practiced knowledge, where we apply them through logical and clear processes. Our skill levels vary in degree based on our natural talent, how we apply it, and repetition of the application.

Early on in life, we began new skills with unrefined talent. With this as a starting point, it is no wonder we felt a bit clunky. Just know that it is normal to feel like we have two left feet when learning new skills. As we practice and improve, we can tack on more knowledge and skills. That is one of the main reasons we experienced refresher training at the beginning of every school year. Students would struggle a lot more with the new year's lessons if they forgot how to apply previous year's skills. After practicing again and through muscle memory, they typically found they can do them more smoothly. When we begin to experience great successes and ENJOY our DANCE, most of us naturally desire to alter or augment it with other skills to personalize it.

A prime example is when we started walking or riding a bike. We wobbled, fell, got back up, and did them again until we finally succeeded. Once we figured it out, we increased our abilities with speed, balance, coordination, etc. From there, the sky was the limit as we ran, jumped, skipped, and performed wheelies, slides, hops, and many other tricks. This same approach is evident in every area of our lives, worthy of our time and effort.

Logically, people who realize, EMBRACE, and hone their natural talent early on tend to have an advantage from the start. Rest assured, if they do not improve upon their innate abilities, more dedicated people will pass them by. As a cross country running coach, I noticed this quite often. Our talented runners who were lackadaisical during practice inevitably fell behind their peers during races. Once they dedicated themselves to training, they would then excel and catch up or surpass fellow runners. As they recognized their talent and felt more encouraged to train harder, their running would launch and they'd experience new personal best times. Not only did they improve, but they also began to have more fun even during intense workouts and more rigorous races.

You apply your skills everywhere in your life because everything VENTURED into has basic skills attached. If you do not have a lot of talent in a particular area of interest and foundational skills, you can learn the basics and practice applying them. After the basic skills are understood, tested, and true, you can bring out those lagging talents, advance the skills, and develop expertise through new steps, tools, and resources. The point here is to stretch yourself. Add skills to your physical, intellectual, emotional, and intuitive knowledge, even if at first it initially feels like you are DANCING with two left feet. You'll get the hang of it!

> *Learn the basics of what you want and EMBRACE that an established standards exist. Adjust according to your feedback or set new standards and press on if you miss the mark.*

Finesse

To finesse your DANCE is to use your talents, knowledge, and skills together in a way that easily flows and is productive. Your DANCE is polished when you lose track of space and time and get lost in your ENJOYMENT. Evidence of your style and grace is seen everywhere through repeated success and steady positive energy. You remain poised and easily use your intuition to choose the best paths and navigate your life with power and finesse!

When you apply your talents to the best of your ability, you know you are DANCING with finesse. If you lack any of the three components of talent, knowledge, or skills, the DANCE will initially feel clunky, unnatural, or maybe a bit awkward. Let's break this down with the runners.

As cross-country season began each year, the runners generally all started at a slower pace and tired quickly. Many of the naturally talented runners took their gift for granted and had not maintained or improved their skills through the summer. Most of the other returning runners often did not practice their new skills and knowledge of form and techniques necessary to excel. Newly joined runners simply did not realize they had talent or lacked basic knowledge and skills of how to run. After a couple of training months and a few races, everyone justifiably improved. With new enhanced foundational talent, they each learned, created, and used strategies to perform their best during the races. The runners who put forth the greatest effort and applied their knowledge and skills developed a DANCE that led them to surpass their best times and competitors. As they advanced, they grew more confident, excited, and eager to run the follow-on races. I use this example because it's easy to see when talents, knowledge, and skills work together to create a DANCE. The same is true for any talent you want to develop. It takes practice and dedication to use them and, for many of them, knowing how to use them wisely.

#68 olympiad – raw talents stay black and white until we enhance them with knowledge and skills. Only then will authentic talents flourish!

The beauty about your DANCE is once you get the basics down and begin to groove, you can always boost the experience by tacking on new knowledge and skills. VENTURING out there with your DANCE can seem intimidating at first, but keep in mind, it is all in the experience you want to create for yourself. Your determination is what makes it come alive. By using your personal power to choose, you can shape it in a manner that offers you the most value and joy over time. The trick is knowing how much and what kind of help you need or prefer in order to bring it out. Slip on your shoes and let's DANCE!

Law of Wisdom – When you use wisdom, you erase karma. Sometimes this can be very painful, but remember, the greater the pain, the faster and deeper you learn.

Freestyle DANCE

One way to finesse your DANCE is by developing and practicing it alone. Based on your experiences, you often know your gaps and what you need to learn. You may pick up and use specific hints and tips from others, but for the most part, you are flying solo. Some examples of Freestyle DANCING include stand-alone courses, deep research, personal development, and even what you learn through reflections in solitude. Self-paced learning and practice offer us independence, flexibility, and deeper insights. This method is how I decided to earn my graduate and post-graduate degrees.

As a busy professional mom, I needed flexibility if I was going to advance my education. Although I could have sat in a schoolhouse, I had other priorities that needed to harmonize with this ADVENTURE. My program type was distance learning, now evolved to online education. It allowed me to do all of my work at home. I would connect with each professor, receive the syllabus, purchase the books, and work through the class independently. It took me 10 years to complete my Bachelor's degree. It was hard! From there, I decided to pursue my Masters' degrees with the same type program and the convenience of the internet. My ability to overcome the combined challenges of flying solo, home priorities, and managing a career, was one of the most rewarding achievements in my life. I gained more than an education, though. Above all, I learned how to honor my values, stay motivated, and harness my RESILIENCE!

Freestyle DANCE may not be for all of us. Books and repetitious actions may not offer enough encouragement for you to hone your DANCE. You may need to borrow motivation, knowledge, and expertise from others, such as coaches, mentors, and counselors, who can help you maximize your strengths. Along with your teachers, these professionals offer enthusiasm, incentives, and guidance to get you started and keep you engaged. Here is where you combine your Freestyle DANCE with a Line DANCE.

Line DANCE

Let's all DANCE together. People moving in the same direction along the same track is called Line DANCING. You each still DANCE independently, yet all follow similar paths, share the same material, and strive to reach common goals. Examples of people Line DANCING include support groups classroom participants, communities of practice, and teams. DANCING with a group can help you discover more talents and develop them through other people's perspectives and feedback. When you commit to Line DANCING, you want to feel motivated, dedicated, and approachable to the group regardless of whether you are paying for it or volunteering. Ultimately, since others rely on you to play your role, your commitment is vital!

#30 humpty-dumpty – sometimes we need help putting things back together. Find and surround yourself with the best people who possess the resources, talent, and your success in mind.

In my executive leadership coach and supervisor roles, I DANCE a variety of Line DANCES with people. I can often tell who will excel quickly and who is just going through the motions. Those who harnessed their talents, focused on putting their best foot forward, and practiced their skills seemed to experience the most significant successes and ENJOYMENT. Those who did not, usually did not commit to the work, the group, or themselves. Most of the time, the person was basically uncertain. As we work together, we overcame their barriers and created new moves to finesse and integrate their DANCE. Although it may sound easy, the path can also be layered with self-imposed limitations. Since we all learn at our own pace, we simply take one step at a time!

Just like Freestyle DANCING, Line DANCING may also not be a good fit for you. Sometimes a group of people can become distracting or even overstimulating, so a more intimate setting may be appropriate. If working with a group doesn't scratch that itch, you can try a different partner, such as a tutor or personal trainer, who has in-depth expertise in your area of interest and can offer personal attention. These professionals offer a fresh perspective and dedicated attention while teaching and encouraging you to reach new heights, even ones you had not previously considered. In the DANCING scene, we will refer to this as Ballroom DANCING!

Ballroom DANCE

A close synergistic partnership or joint effort is comparable to Ballroom, Ballet, or Swing DANCING. It is where people with similar talents partner and rely on one another to sharpen their knowledge and skills together. This DANCE is more collaborative and intimate in nature. Each can only practice so much alone and is incomplete without the other person to perform their role. Examples of Ballroom DANCES are those steps we do with a spouse, business partner, coach, mentor, teammate, activity partner, healer, etc. You join together with the other person and work toward the same goal. Here, you each have an opportunity to use your talents, but you must continuously refine your knowledge so you can DANCE well together. This DANCE can be the most intense practice and certainly the most rewarding.

Just like all DANCES, Ballroom DANCING has its challenges. One of the most widespread is that people can completely lose themselves in each other. At first, that may seem okay, but when either person needs space to grow or wants to DANCE solo, the partnership may suffocate. Therefore, be careful of constraining influences that do not allow the other person to express their DANCE. You'll step on each other's toes. It can be painful, create scars, and wreck the harmonious DANCE altogether. Each person must stay light, solid, and fluid on their own feet while stepping harmoniously with one another.

The other challenge is when one partner outgrows the other. In the beginning, you DANCE very well together and ENJOY learning and creating. When either of you stops progressing, both will find it challenging to perform the DANCE moves together. One may feel inadequate, and the other may become bored or frustrated. This divergence can lead to disaster and the inevitable end of your intimate Ballroom DANCE. We see both of these problems quite often in marriages, businesses, and jobs. Regardless of the ADVENTURE, if you want your DANCE to work together, both partners must be willing to tweak their steps and move in unison!

As you lean into your unique steps and are open to your partner's moves, you can co-create a DANCE together that works well and allows you to flow together. When Freestyle, Line, and Ballroom DANCING do not seem to work, sometimes you need to just DANCE with what you have. Just DANCE!

Law of Fellowship - Our energy is multiplied when we work together.

Just DANCE

All in all, each of us needs to discover ways to use our DANCE effectively. This idea is especially true when you AWAKEN to what you do well, what you get lost in, and what drives you. You will know it because your DANCE energizes you. It gives you a sense of strength, vitality, and smoothness unmatched by other activities. It just feels right, inspires you, and most of the time gets you the results you want. It also can be a bit scary when you VENTURE out there to give it your best shot. But don't worry. You will accomplish amazing feats when done with care and intention.

Whether you fly solo or with others, EMBRACE your DANCE fully! Also, be aware that it is critical for you to use your DANCE at the correct times and in the right places. Since each person has their own DANCE, lack of awareness or appreciation of these differences can lead to misunderstandings and unwanted feedback. Remember, you have freewill and can use your willpower to perform your DANCE however you want and so does everyone else. By recognizing the strengths of others and the value each brings, you can better see where yours complements or competes with others. Our DANCES should allow for flexibility, variety, and freedom as they come with diverse views, ideas, and perspectives. Instead of rivaling, take this as a perfect opportunity to be open-minded, learn, and enhance your own DANCE from what you ENJOY in theirs. The person with the greatest flexibility is the one that stands in the best light. So, lean on your DANCES and pick the ideal one for each situation.

An easy way to tell if your DANCE aligns with your surroundings is by paying attention to how other people interact with you. They offer great clues as to how well you are using it. If you come on too strong, intimidating, overbearing, or the opposite and experience unwanted attention or rejection, that is your sign to change up your steps a bit or shift to another DANCE. The point isn't to conform, but more so to use your DANCE wisely to get the most out of it.

For instance, one of my talents is responsibility. I am very good at taking responsibility for and ownership of my own actions. In the past, when others did not do the same, I found that their carelessness and negligence would zap my emotions. To avoid that zap, I would take the initiative and handle other people's responsibilities. Ultimately, instead of facing my emotions, I'd physically burn myself out. I became aware of this after quite a few coaching sessions. I now have a better understanding that people will learn through complacency just as well as failure. Although I still feel the pull (inspired) to help, I realize that everyone is responsible for their own actions. This has helped me build a better relationship with myself and the people important to me by knowing what is mine to do. I may not always get it right, but I DANCE the best I can!

We always have a choice to wing our DANCE and adjust our moves as we go or find somewhere else to DANCE. You do not have to stop or conform, but merely become aware if your strengths fit or if they are in unwanted, wasted, or ineffective spaces. Lack of awareness is like slam dancing in a room with two-steppers or, in everyday terms, working a detail-oriented job as a visionary. You will not only stumble; you will know right away what feels awkward and generates unwanted reactions. Create your own trend and make space to test your DANCE until you know where it works well. In your **Zone of Potential**, this is called "flow with the go." Find where you flow at your best and go there! In your own space and unique way, you use your strengths to create the best experience possible. It is all part of being AWAKE to your surroundings and how you authentically come into the world.

> ⚡ *DANCE like only you know how! Nobody knows your DANCE like you. Use it wisely and watch how your VENTURES begin to take root!*

In order to use your DANCES with confidence, creativity, and finesse, you must practice - practice - practice! All situations offer opportunities to perfect any one of your DANCE moves. The key here is to identify which works best for the situation, be flexible with your steps, and not overdo it. This approach will allow you to use your strengths, deal with your weaknesses, and navigate challenging circumstances with flow. As you become more intentional with them, watch how your VENTURES flourish!

VENTURE

*T*he word VENTURE gets such a bad rap. Just the word itself sounds so unnerving for some of us. What does it actually mean to VENTURE? Exactly what it suggests; to risk, dare, or try something new. Merely placing your feet on the floor in the morning comes with risk. And, while we VENTURE into new and routine activities every single day, we do not necessarily do it blindly. Most of the time, we subconsciously consider risks based on our intention, habits, and intuition. In Failing Forward, John C. Maxwell states, "Risk must be evaluated not by the fear it generates in you or the probability of your success, but by the value of the goal."

The point is not that we don't VENTURE randomly or aimlessly. It's that we have a tough time with assessing the impact of risks beforehand. Insurance agencies and other legal bindings offer us some help in that arena. We have the opportunity to purchase various types of policies to offset the potential risks of VENTURES in every part of our lives. Life, health, auto, business, financial, and even pet insurance among many others, help reduce the angst of uncertainty and make accident expenses more manageable. With protection, we can more confidently decide if the risk is ultimately worth the reward.

One of the most significant reasons people struggle with VENTURING is the physical, mental, and emotional barriers that cannot be resolved with money. Just the thought of the possible pain stops many of us in our tracks. It is these barriers that we must face if we want to grow and create a life worthy of getting up in the morning. In Japan, anything worth getting out of bed for is called our ***ikigai***. As you examine how you maneuver through daily routines, you'll discover how life is synchronized to encourage risk-taking aligned with your ikigai. Over time you may even begin to get more curious about what's possible and relax a little when VENTURING into new activities and the unknown.

The Big Picture

VENTURING into something new begins with seeing the big picture — with yourself as the main character! Some people stay small and play the extras in their own stories and movies. They have such a tough time seeing themselves as the star. They go into work, do the same job, and come home to the same routine. They regularly watch the same television shows and have the same types of conversations with the same people in their lives. They feel efficient, well-structured, and super organized. There is nothing wrong with that. It is what got them to where they are today. But who you are today is not who you have to be tomorrow!

It's not uncommon for us to want more or even just something different. Yet, we find ourselves stuck in our same routines and habits. As everything around us continues to change, our once-efficient actions eventually become less effective. Many will continue in the same old ruts because they're comfortable. For others, it becomes monotonous, boring, and even mind-numbing. They lose sight of their big picture as they begin to question their ability to change or reach lofty goals. But really, it all starts with one small step, one small action, one small gesture, one small VENTURE based on one big picture!

When our lives become unimaginative and dull, we tend to crave excitement, something more, and anything that will spark our creativity. When you are clear on what you want and intentionally choose the VENTURE, the unexpected events will be less unsettling and easier to understand how they feed into your life. When you start with the big picture and the end in mind, you will be better prepared to tackle obstacles and know they are worth the effort. With these fundamentals, you will be certain to know you are on a path to make life your favorite ADVENTURE.

You can choose VENTURES that produce incredible experiences when you stop allowing everything around you to affect you. Be willing to commit your time, energy, and space to prepare for what is to come. Although a plan can help, you don't always need extensive planning. You simply need to imagine what you want and take small, calculated steps to get there. It may feel uneasy at first, but remember, you take risks every day in everything you do. Do it methodically with purpose, passion, and intention, and watch how your experiences unfold.

Slow to Go

As you VENTURE out there, it's normal to want a sense of confidence that your choices are as logical and realistic as possible. Generating a positive feeling can be a challenge if you have tried similar things in the past and didn't get what you expected. Uncertainty may have clouded your choices. Not very many people feel confident enough to take chances unless results are practically guaranteed. These types of situations can make our stress factors rise while decreasing our ability to think creatively. With an inhibited creativity level, you may start to think you are defeated, feel hopeless, and not take those first steps. Yet all is not lost! It's a matter of slowing down and giving yourself some time to decompress. This is your opportunity to discover more options, tap into your dreams, and develop visions of what you want.

> *Slow down. Visualize where your VENTURE will lead you in the end and you will quickly know the difference between a fantasy and your reality.*

There is plenty of debate about whether or not we should follow our dreams. I invite you to consider this idea for a moment. Nothing created came about without a dream, vision, or image. Nothing! That is not to say you should pursue all of your dreams. It is whether your dreams reflect your true desires or are merely an envious or frivolous fantasy.

The way to know if your dream is a fantasy is whether you are willing to do what it takes to make it come true. You have to see yourself in the actual experience. It must inspire and motivate you to take action. But be cautious. If you dream of a big house on a hill simply because someone else has one, you may not want to do what it takes to get it or care for it. See yourself inside of it and maintaining it or handing out money for someone else to maintain it. If this does not feel appealing, your dream may simply be a wonderful fantasy. In contrast, if you genuinely want it for yourself and your family, you will see yourself living in it and NURTURING it when you get it.

#7 astronaut – get out of your head and beyond this world to dream big. Eyes wide open or shut, look up to the enormity of the sky, feel its energy, and dream. Bring those visions back to Earth and live your own life!

The challenge with uncovering the big picture is that it can be difficult to capture it in a vision. We are constantly going and doing and often forget to use our imaginations as we did when we were kids. When you take a moment to slow down, you will be able to see what is really going on in your life. You will begin to visualize possibilities of how you can use your personal power to honor your values and use your DANCE. Brought together, this will allow you to limit your misguided activities and start harmonizing actions that follow your dreams instead. By the way, dreams do not only arrive while you sleep. Daydream, meditate, contemplate, or use other restful practices anytime throughout your day. Once again, you just need to be willing and do it!

As you break away from the daily grind to expand your mind, you become more deliberate with choices and decision-making. Your big picture becomes more distinct, and you worry less about missteps and focus more on benefits. This clarity also makes it easier to see what already supports your vision. Once you reach that point, you will realize you are already on your way.

Keep it real. Keep it right. Hold onto your dreams with wonder and awe as they offer you signs from within!

Starter Kit

When we VENTURE into any activity, we may feel ill-prepared or ill-equipped, like we lack sufficient skills or support. Similar to most people, you don't want to waste time, money, and effort. Consider these three key factors to ensure your starter kit is in place: your stuff, encouragement, and your beliefs. You may end up dragging your feet if any of these three areas lack sufficient support. Therefore, to begin any ADVENTURE with confidence, you will undoubtedly want resources and people that can and will support you, along with your own helpful thoughts, to kick you into action.

Once you have taken inventory of what you already own, you may feel a sense of confidence, surety, and clarity. But that will not last long if your cluttered world gets in the way. Many of us hold onto unhelpful, useless, and outdated things, relationships, and beliefs. If you want something different, then it is time for you to identify what bogs you down and clear it out. These impediments will invariably stand in the way of your ADVENTURE. To move forward and maintain momentum, decide what still offers value and clear out the rest to make space for what really matters.

Where do you start? This challenge is why your big picture is so important. If you do not step back and visualize what you want, your focus will be all over the place, and you may struggle to notice the many treasures at your fingertips. These resources can kick you into action when they bring back familiar memories and reignite the pleasures once experienced.

First consider your belongings. Many of us fill our closets with clothing and shoes that haven't seen the light of day for quite some time. We have kept outdated equipment, tools, and sports gear that we intended to fix but never did. We have kitchen gadgets galore, silverware stuffed in drawers, and plasticware crammed in cabinets that beg for use. Our jackets and coats that once had purposes now hang senselessly in hall closets or by the door. We fill our shelves with dusty books, magazines, and manuals that we neglect for what might seem like forever. You get the point. Yet, most of us lug all of this stuff with us with the hopes of using it again.

Some of our things are well used and worn down for obvious reasons. Others are in mint condition because they are either well-maintained or underused. And then we have some stuff that may still have price tags or plastic covers on them because we never used them at all. We see this all of the time with exercise equipment and outgrown toys. Well, here is your opportunity to break it all out to see if and how they fit into your current and desired lifestyle.

When inspecting what you have, take care not to bog yourself down with faulty or outdated items. They can lead to frustration and procrastination. Also, be careful not to ditch items that will work for the short term to get you moving. If temporary use is your route, consider safety the most critical deciding factor. Check everything for fit, usefulness, and suitability, like rips, tears, rust, decay, mildew, broken and missing pieces, etc. Pick it up, test it out, and determine if it is something that can help you get started. If it is safe and makes sense to use it, use it. Repair, donate, or toss the rest out altogether. Doing so will make space for your dreams to flourish!

Now determine what needs to be replaced, upgraded, or newly included in the experience. As a bonus, this newness will be like treating yourself before you even start. It is comparable to giving yourself a tip (transaction in progress) or reward. Incentives can be the key to your motivation. Do not allow a lack of resources an excuse to procrastinate. Get the necessities you need upfront. Do your research, ask knowledgeable friends, make a list, and acquire your new items so you can have the best experience possible. Not everything will be expensive, and you don't need all of the bells and whistles to start. Find items gently used or on sale. Graciously accept donations. Just make sure it is functional and can help.

The next closet to address is the closet of people in your life. For the most part, you intuitively know who will either encourage you or drag you down. Certain people can offer helpful insights into what they see. They can let you know what they notice about activities you do well and which ones challenge you. Just keep in mind that they will do so from their perspective and may have their own physical, mental, or emotional barriers. People who love you act and speak with good intentions. They naturally want to help you be triumphant and feel good about it. It's just that some people do not see the same value or joy that you do from your eyes. Knowing what motivates them can be helpful when considering their opinions!

Deliberately surround yourself with the ideal people in your personal and professional life who will support and encourage your new endeavor. If it's knowledge or skills you lack to start, seek experts who will offer basic steps. For encouragement, tap into your family and friends who are always there for you and want to see you succeed. Many people want to see us prosper and experience the same for themselves. That is why so many support groups exist. Join one and share in the motivation, fellowship, and encouragement to get you on the right track. As you do, keep in mind that everyone is still on their own path and has their own idea of what they want to experience. Pick and choose wisely.

My brother, Rocky, is one such family member who wants to see all of his brothers and sisters succeed. He has helped me many times with his expertise. When I decided I wanted a website for my coaching business, I didn't know where to start and was overwhelmed. Like most of my family members with computer questions, I reached out to Rocky for help as he had been providing excellent IT services and designing websites for years. He made some recommendations and offered to build my site. Beyond setting up the site, he also provided security services and ensured my work email flowed to other applications. Rocky took from his personal time to teach me about running a website and continues to ensure I am settled with my technology. With such support and encouragement, I knew Rocky was the precise person to ask.

In contrast, a very close friend said that I should not maintain such a muscular build. Jack confidently stated that my muscles would turn to fat and become flabby. I could have received this in various ways and been offended, but I had a good idea of what he meant. I toyed with him a little bit when I kindly informed him that biologically muscle does not turn to fat. I also told him that I basically understood what he was trying to convey. Jack was suggesting that, as I aged, my muscles would become less toned, smaller, and hang in my skin if I ever stopped working out. He was going through the aging experience himself and did not want me to 'suffer' the same as I grew older. I assumed his motivation was that of care, yet my values overrode his beliefs. I did not remove Jack from my life just because his perspective was different from mine. I simply EMBRACED a different viewpoint, THANKED him, and continued along my fitness ADVENTURE without further mention.

Take inventory of your relationships and decide what to do with the ones that have held you back or take all of your time. Be aware of the nay-sayers, negative Nancys, and time thieves who detract you from your VENTURE. When you free yourself from these types of folks, you can make space for new relationships with people who believe in you, support you, and maybe even partner with you. It can be exciting to make new friends, build new relationships, and share new experiences together. Many people want the same ADVENTURE as you. Make space for and encourage them, too!

The last cluttered closet contains beliefs. If you have all of the tools and people and still are hesitant to take that first step, you may want to create new beliefs. You might be wondering why beliefs are important to start, but trust me, they are. Sometimes we get trapped in old belief systems, especially regarding our abilities. They have served the purposes of keeping you safe, protecting your values, and getting you where you are today. You see, our beliefs can have us running away in fear or stuck in our muck. Who knows, you may fear what comes after success or failure. It takes faith to know you can do whatever it is you want. That does not mean fake it until you make it. It means to prepare, focus, and have the courage to take the leap!

Our beliefs also have a tendency to kick us into action. As you become aware of beliefs that move you in an unwanted direction, you can purposely develop new ones that help you move on a more desired path. You only do what you believe. If it is something you sincerely want to do, you will find a way to make it happen. Success is the outcome that proves you did it. Failure is simply feedback telling you to try something different. Take inventory of your belief system so you can identify how they affect your VENTURE. Try on new ones and validate them through small wins or big ones.

People perform phenomenal and inspiring feats because they simply believe they can and take steps to make it happen. The shortest National Basketball Association player was 5 foot 3 inches tall. He surely had to believe in himself and his abilities to compete with players who were two whole feet taller than him and could jump up to 48 inches in the air. MotoGP motorcycle riders hit speeds of 200 miles per hour and take turns at 180 miles per hour. One slip of confidence when handling their crotch rocket could lead to a devastating outcome. They all had to start with an innate desire to do these activities and a belief that they could.

We frequently see inspiring feats from people with disabilities, too. A person with a disability can be anyone born with physical or mental conditions or those drastically afflicted by tragic life events, such as wounded combat veterans. They must believe they can effectively function in life with their disability. Many learn to overcome obstacles with walking, running, speaking, social functioning, etc. to become productive contributors to society. They indeed must have a deep belief in themselves and the willpower to do what they want regardless of their limitations. These may be extreme cases, but they are necessary to illustrate how our beliefs play a massive role in taking risks.

When you genuinely believe you can and want to do something, you will find a way to do it. If instead, you have doubts, fears, or apprehensions, you will keep putting off the first crucial steps by not doing anything at all or make excuses to do something else. You sabotage your VENTURE with the coulda, shoulda, woulda thoughts, and feelings of regret that emerge. With solid and supportive beliefs and faith in your abilities, you too can experience miraculous achievements!

Routine Adjustments

As closet clearing moves along, you can begin to determine how to harmonize it all into your daily activities. We are often reluctant to taking on experiences vastly different from what we are accustomed. As you AWAKEN to what you have been doing, you may notice some of your current activities already support what you want. With this in mind, unaccustomed activities might not seem so large, difficult, or complex.

Here is an example relevant for many of us. If you want a specific pet and grapple with how to manage caring for it, you may be hesitant to get the one you want. To make the decision a little easier, consider your knowledge of what you do now in the basic areas of feeding, watering, cleaning, health care, and companionship and how you can apply it to this experience. From there, you can research a little more and decide if the effort is worth integrating into your lifestyle. With an investment in the care and affection of your pets, they will be your best friends forever.

Before denying yourself an ADVENTURE, visualize it as part of your life. The beauty in starting is we don't have to figure it out all at once. Even the smallest experiences can bring us satisfaction and happiness. Consider what you are already doing. If you see evidence that what you want will harmonize with your current activities, you will feel more prepared and confident in your decision. You will also be more compelled to adjust your lifestyle accordingly.

Law of Ritual – Any action you intentionally repeated becomes a rite. It strengthens through self-empowerment, any external power you allow into it, and the combined energy of both.

Another challenge could be habits and rituals. We developed these routines to help keep us on track, yet they may also have a tendency to get in our way of a new experience. Sometimes we need to shake up our way of life to allow for something greater. We also lean on unproductive routines that waste time and energy. We respond to other people's little whims, watch excessive TV, surf the internet, or find ourselves on our cell phones with social media or reading email all day long. Most of the time, it is because we are looking for immediate gratification, belonging, or excitement. As we become comfortable with these activities, we continue to go back to them and often become reliant on them. This world of fantasy can stop us from experiencing the real deal!

> *Make space on your calendar for you. Place your most valuable activities high on your priority list and do something for them at least three times a week.*

The first step in changing routines is identifying which ones no longer serve you or are unproductive. Use what you know to start a new habit and make it a priority. It's never that we do not have the time for new ADVENTURES. We simply do not allocate time to make new experiences a higher priority. One ENJOYABLE aspect about life is testing new ways to do things and learning what works.

My belief system often plays with me as I consider new VENTURES for my coaching business. At one point, I wanted to start an ADVENTURE called Wisdom Walks. This event included hiking or walking with self-discovery questions and a treasure hunt for people wanting to learn a little more about themselves while ENJOYING the great outdoors. I was unsure how to include it into my schedule or how many people, if any, would like to join. Everything else seemed more important as I allowed my doubts to power over my desire. My daily routine at that point was easy, and I filled space in my schedule with anything but creating the Wisdom Walks. Yet the desire for these hikes still burned inside. I knew I would ENJOY them, so I decided to alter my mindset and create them for me and anyone else who wanted to join. That did the trick. I stopped playing with my phone and filled the empty space on my calendar with activities to develop a gameplan and kick off the ADVENTURE. I had fun creating, scheduling, and running each event. Sometimes two people showed up and other times ten. As an aside, the Wisdom Walks successfully met five of my set goals; fitness, business, social, family, and self-development.

We've all heard or experienced stories similar to this one, but each of us needs to decide what activities stand in our way of what we truly want. Sometimes just by changing one little detail with your stuff, relationships, or actions, you can start something better. But it does not stop there. As you make way for your VENTURE, consider what you will intentionally do with time that frees on your calendar so you continue to positively impact your entire life. There is something to be said for new beginnings.

You can apply these concepts to every aspect of your life. It's about knowing what you have, making space for what you do not, and incorporating new things, people, and beliefs to support what you want. That's how you take your first steps to VENTURE into any new experience with more certainty and confidence. If, after you look at the big picture, you are still not stepping out, consider putting together your own personal SWOT. This tool can help you look at your vision a little differently. With a SWOT, you can pinpoint your current strengths and weaknesses to determine if what you want is genuinely for you. As part of this process, you also create ideas to capitalize on opportunities and manage or mitigate potential barriers. Come on, let's SWOT this to get your party started!

SWOT It

It is one thing to dream about the big picture, but if you do not make a decision to act, it will never become your reality. Many decision tools exist, but the personal SWOT analysis is one of the most effective tools you can use to make wise decisions. SWOT stands for Strengths, Weaknesses, Opportunities, and Threats. Strengths and weaknesses are all about you. Opportunities and threats are those other people, things, and events that may impact your success. Most business professionals use this tool to better understand what they possess to leverage new opportunities and foresee what may get in their way. When you think about it, many aspects of life and business are very similar. They both have relationships, daily operations, money needs, personal development, and so on. By using your personal SWOT, you can align your strengths with opportunities for a great experience. You can also figure out what you are not encouraged to do and reduce the potential problems. When you complete the SWOT, it will offer you greater personal insights and self-assurance to take action.

Strengths

We love to use our strengths. As covered in the DANCE chapter, they are the finesse of your physical, mental, and emotional traits wrapped in your talents, knowledge, and skills to make up your unique DANCE. Remember, your DANCE has a direct association to your values. Because they do, you will feel more energized and positive when you lean on them. When you consider your strengths in the SWOT, you must be really honest with yourself. Take care not to confuse your passions with your strengths. For example, you may be passionate about having your voice heard which might lead you to think you are strong at public speaking. At first you might be in over your head speaking to large audiences. Instead, you may want to choose smaller, more intimate settings where you can experience success and excel. As you develop your style and gain experience, your DANCE will develop. By better understanding your strengths, you will become clearer and make more calculated decisions. As a result, you will feel a sense of purpose, confidence, and self-control.

Weaknesses

We all have weaknesses, regardless of how strong people seem to appear. Weaknesses are things we do not do well because we are not invested in improving them nor practicing them. Because of this, they wear us out, drain us, and tax our ability to stay the course. The caution here is to not confuse your weakness with a lack of knowledge and skills. Not one person is good at everything, but all circumstances offer us chances to develop. Without proactively recognizing and addressing weaknesses ahead of time, you will find it difficult to reach your goals. The point here is to not allow your weaknesses to stop you from your true desires.

Test your weaknesses to determine what drains you. This is not about taking out the trash or daily mundane chores, although they can also be included. It is about sifting through people, items, and activities in your past that led you to doubt your abilities and stop you from wanting to start. How can you tell the difference between your strengths and weaknesses? Most of the time, it's pretty easy. When you are using your strengths, you end up being satisfied and excited even if you are fatigued. Your weaknesses give you a feeling of dread and insecurity. They drain you of your energy, and you do not look forward to doing them. Procrastination is a key factor in identifying your weaknesses.

Keep in mind that procrastination is only an indicator, not the overall answer. To validate your weakness, question why you delay the activity. The answers you receive will help you decide whether to improve in that area or recognize it as something for someone else to do and let it go. This decision offers you space to focus on your values and generates a sense of ease by minimizing what zaps your energy. As an added benefit, by EMBRACING your weaknesses, you extend the opportunity for someone else to express their strengths.

Learning about yourself can be exciting. As you continue to capture your strengths and weaknesses, you will gain a deeper understanding of how to operate at your best when you begin. Your personal potential will unfold, and barriers will reveal themselves. Considering your individual strengths and weaknesses is essential when you start anything. By understanding them, you can look for further opportunities to use your strengths and build confidence to take those first steps. As you start looking at your external world of opportunities and threats, you will be better positioned to identify how your experience may impact your life and the lives of others. Who knows, you may become more enthusiastic and feel an urge to VENTURE sooner.

Opportunities

We have so many opportunities to consider in our lives. When we are not sure what we want, we will find it really hard to choose which ones to take. As you AWAKEN to who you are and what is important to you, you'll start seeing opportunities arise that are appropriate according to your desires. Why? Where your focus goes, your attention grows. And, where your attention goes, your focus grows. If your focus is scattered, you will become overwhelmed by so many opportunities and bright shiny objects. You will wonder which ones to pursue. When you begin to make purposeful choices, your decisions will become easier, clearer, and quicker. You will notice people, things, and events that can help you VENTURE into action. You'll discover similarities, trends, and how your talents stand out. You will consciously and intuitively position yourself to enhance your experiences. Remember, any chance you can apply your DANCE is an opportunity to experience your true and authentic self.

With a clear focus on what you want, new opportunities will appear. As you take advantage of these opportunities, like most of us, you will likely want your path to be as smooth and flowing as possible. Bear in mind, sometimes that may not be the case. Many opportunities come with plenty of obstacles that may cause you to rethink your decision. Get to know what they may be so they do not come as an unpleasant surprise later. The unknown is like a vacuum that can suck up fictitious stories of fear. Deny your power to these stories and be impartial about them when they arise. Don't avoid them, ignore them, react to them, or give them your energy. Consider that ignorance is only bliss if you realize obstacles can still exist even when you are not experiencing them. Be indifferent to them so they do not stop you from seizing suitable opportunities for you. Tackle them!

Law of Fearful Confrontation – When you face and do what you fear, you will likely feel more courageous and satisfied. You may even generate an internal rush and a desire to do it again.

Threats

External influences and situations always exist and can potentially challenge your desire to VENTURE that first step or leap. As you pay attention to what was and is happening in the world around you, you will soon detect who and what may threaten your outcome. The past really can inform the future. It's cyclical. If you don't change what you're thinking, feeling, and doing, a similar person or experience will have a tendency to come around and bite again.

Maybe you are surrounded and influenced by nay-sayers or people who would be jealous of your success. This is not about competition, but rather realizing that you bring unique value to the table. Your strengths set you apart from everyone else. Just because someone has an opinion about you or what you do does not mean it has merit. As stated before, people come with their perspectives from their own experiences. At the same time, it also does not mean you shouldn't hear them. Not all people with opposing ideas are a threat. Those who have observed you long enough will see trends in what you say and do that may stop you from your VENTURE. Use their insights to honestly verify it for yourself and test their validity, but not to scare you away. If you do not surround yourself with honest, supportive people, you may suffer from poor feedback or advice. People's input can either help you think it through or stop you from ever starting.

Objects are typically less of a threat to your livelihood than people and events. Often these types of threats are associated with a lack of equipment, money, or time. As addressed earlier, this can be tackled by knowing what you have available. From your inventory, you may have discovered that you need much more than you initially expected. Simply remember, VENTURE means to start. You do not need to have everything at the start. Work with the materials you have, budget wisely for the future, and carve out a little time for you to take the first steps. Doing so will be helpful to keep you focused and organized. By knowing which materials you lack, you can better prepare to develop options to obtain them along the way and adjust when troubles arise.

The biggest type of threats to any new VENTURE is events. You will almost certainly be hit with unexpected events. Identifying what you think could go wrong may ease your hesitance to begin by lessening the potential sting of surprise. In this way, you can prepare for what may come later without allowing the circumstances to hinder your start. Be careful not to sabotage your experience through anticipation; simply be aware to prepare.

Your SWOT might seem a bit difficult to assess at first. Just remember, we always face uncomfortable feelings when we VENTURE into new territory. The idea is not to focus on right or wrong, but rather on whether you made the best choice. If you feel distressed, anxious, or agony in your weaknesses or threats, realize that they are just areas that require your attention, love, and support. You can build your SWOT as simple or detailed as you like. By using it for decisions from the start, you will feel more well-informed and poised because you are ready to prepare, plan, and act. You can now break your big picture into smaller steps, so you can start your VENTURE rationally and with structure.

Start Small

Sometimes life can seem so big, unwieldy, and cumbersome. You may be caught up in all of the details and "what ifs" that can overwhelm you. But think about it for a minute. When you look back at all of the most difficult yet highly successful experiences in your lifetime, you might have found them initially huge, complex, and consuming. Most of us do, because anything worth doing will seem that way. But your success comes from breaking a new endeavor into bite-sized chunks. Start with the end in mind by working backward from your goal, preparing, and maybe even making a plan. Use your SWOT to maximize your ability to stay focused. By knowing how you want the ADVENTURE to finish, choosing how to get there, and using internal/external awareness, you will feel less anxious about the enormity of fulfilling your vision and ENJOY it even more.

Aspire with Goals

As you prepare, your ADVENTURE will be well-served if you set clear goals. Without goals, your aspirations will remain dreams. Jim Rohn put it brilliantly. The ultimate reason to set goals is to entice you to become the person it takes to achieve them. Your goal is not a pass, fail, or any grade. It is a tool to help you develop and track your progress.

Goals can be as simple or complex as you wish, but the simpler and more specific they are, the easier you can use them. They should be something you can envision yourself being, having, and doing. Write them down and say them aloud as if you have already achieved them. Ensure your goals are realistic and responsible to yourself and toward others. Set a date or a few dates to help keep you on track. Align it with your "why" that ties to one of your values so you can feel the pull to complete it and keep the energy alive. Once you've got your goal down, start behaving like it is already part of your life.

Here are three examples of big-picture goals that may require preparation and maybe some planning with smaller goals.

If you want to retire: I am retired at 68 years old. I have the flexibility and freedom to volunteer, visit family, and develop social connections with those who share my same interests. (This goal can impact every area of your life, so preparations and smaller goal-setting are essential.)

If you want a nursing job: I am a registered nurse. My job is fulfilling. I have enriching challenges, a pleasant atmosphere, and an income that I deserve. (Since this goal touches many areas of your life beyond business and career, smaller goals will be helpful. You will also want to be aware of the impact it may have on those areas, including finances, wellness, social, growth, self-image, and possibly even your family.)

If you are working toward learning more about finances: I am a part of a financial social meetup group starting this year. I manage my money better through support and different perspectives. (This is a short-term goal that can be accomplished immediately with little preparation, outside of researching the group and testing the connections.)

Notice the clarity, the alignment with values, and simplicity in each. These goals offer flexibility which lessens the anxiety of following a tight plan. After you capture your goal, break it down into smaller steps as necessary so you can keep track of your progress. These smaller steps also help you stay focused and intentional on what you do and when.

Law of Simplicity – Simplicity brings order to chaos.

Time Travel

If your goals seem a bit scary and overwhelming at first, relax. The big picture is still there, and, unless you're proficient with a crystal ball, you will never really know with certainty how it will turn out anyway. You can turn any delays you encounter into the perfect opportunity to contemplate how you want your ADVENTURE to proceed. Just stay focused and set milestones as markers to get you there. If you struggle with staying focused, break those milestones down a little further and take one step at a time.

Planning out all of these steps and milestones may seem like too much work at first, but the investment of time is worth it. The intent is to create smooth experiences and expose opportunities. If it still seems like

#69 the dream – dreams are the passageway to your inner self. Open the door and you will find a whole new world!

drudgery, step back and shift your mindset. Take a break, use your imagination, and daydream to envision what you want to do next. Each time you do, include as many of your senses as you can. Remember, your five senses are what help you create your reality. When you use them, it is like you can "time travel" to the actual event. This invites you to experience it before it even happens. For example, all of us have had dreams where it seemed like we were there, in person. We clearly saw visions and heard sounds and voices. Sometimes the dream is so real that we actually feel, taste, and smell things in our surroundings. Intentional daydreaming is no different, except you control the dream. Create the whole experience just the way you want it! How cool is that? You will soon discover new details and can break things down into smaller manageable goals. Take in as many specifics as you can and jot them down so you do not forget. The next trick will be to breathe air into it.

When I retired from the military, I made a very bold statement that turned into a lofty goal. I said that I would retire the second time before I was 55 years old. That idea was quite intimidating as my pension was small for an enlisted military person. Money was not the only factor. I wasn't quite sure what would be next for me. To me, retiring did not mean a life of staying home, going fishing, going to the gym, and going back home. I wanted to put my time and effort into my own business and be financially independent while doing so. That meant paying off my house, building a nest egg, and not working a day job for someone else. For 12-13 years, that is exactly what I did. The dream was attainable and I VENTURED in with a plan and loose expectations. I began paying down my house and made some pension moves to support my future lifestyle. At year 11, things seemed to line up for me to become a trained, experienced, and certified leadership coach. Year 12, I opened my own business and began gaining business experience. I was on my way! When year 13 came around, I paid off my home, quit my day job, and focused entirely on scoping and scaling my business. I reached my vision by setting many goals with milestones and keeping focused, flexible, and realistic – relaxed and intentional!

My story is simple, and yet every one of us has done this in some past areas of our lives. The idea is to carefully plan out scenarios and make purposeful choices to make those scenarios come to life. Things may not go exactly as anticipated, but at least you will have a better idea of who and what is needed to start moving toward your life aspirations. The sky is the limit! Use your imagination freely and easily to start making life your favorite ADVENTURE, one baby step at a time.

A Prepared Mind

The way we approach our life often depicts how we will experience success or failure. You see, you act the way you think and feel. Many of our well-developed behavior patterns can be so hard to change. In reality, you do not have to change everything. Many of your routine activities and attitudes will benefit your ability to start something new. By starting small, you can recognize what actions, thoughts, and feelings are helpful and which ones need slight changes. In some cases, even the most trivial changes can feel refreshing like you are starting with a clean slate.

One way to determine if your actions and attitudes will help you get started is to pick any one of your goals and ask yourself why you do not already have it. If you own up to your answer as something you have yet to complete and are willing to get it done, you are likely on the right track. If you find you blame others, you may want to consider adjusting your mindset. You can change many of your circumstances, things in your surroundings, and how you handle events, but you will struggle to change how others approach life. As you consider how your own thoughts and feelings have been driving what you do and what happens as a result, you may soon discover a different truth. This assessment can guide you to VENTURE on with your thoughts, feelings, and actions that work and alter ones you determine will keep you stuck.

Let's use relationships as an example. Better relationships begin with changes in the ways each of us, as a single person, thinks and feels to create actions and words. The first thing couples often do when things go awry is point the finger at others. They claim the other person made them feel or behave in certain ways. Although those feelings happen, each person is responsible for their own triggered thoughts and actions that shaped the outcome. If those same thoughts and actions work well over time, they will continue to use them. This is one of the many little tricks we picked up from our childhood. Remember when you didn't get what you wanted and became upset? You may have yelled, thrown a fit, or cried until you got it. Quite often, it worked! As children, we kept trying different tactics and testing what works. As you grew older, you discovered new ways appropriate to your social environment to get what you wanted. As adults, we get stuck in our ways and seem to forget we have other options. We tend to become overwhelmed or complacent and create patterns or habits to fight or conform to our surroundings. After a while, change becomes even more difficult.

You can apply this approach to every aspect of your life. Your old, worn-out, habitual ways of thinking and feeling have kept you right where you are. If you think, feel, and act the same way, we all know that you can anticipate the same type of results from the same people and in the same circumstances. It is absurd to think otherwise. Once again, gradual small steps to adjust these patterns will help. To top it off, you can start with any of the three: action, feeling, or thought. If you want to start exercising, put on athletic shoes or get to the gym. If you want to save money, start feeling like it is an investment for your future and you are worth it. If you want a new job, start considering what you love about the job you have and what would make it better. By describing in detail how it will look and the feelings it will generate when you have it, you will be better prepared to know if what appears is what you actually wanted.

With small improvements in your thoughts, feelings, and actions, over time you will stop making excuses, have more clarity and confidence, and gain some quick wins in your next steps. To VENTURE is not about having everything at once. It is about preparing your mind for what you will do and attract. By preparing yourself physically, mentally, and emotionally, your mind will focus on your goals consistently.

As you reflect on the example above, recognize that people at the gym - or anywhere - will look at you no matter what, sometimes strangely. Identify any uncomfortable feelings you may have about experiencing that. Now, shift your focus to those who are not looking at you. Notice that most of the people around you are doing their own thing. They are not concerned about you unless you are purposely or unconsciously attracting their attention in some way. To prepare your mind, if you are not trying to be noticed, consider that those who do watch you typically have their own feelings of insecurity and need some type of validation. That is their journey, so let go of it! Instead, create small actions to focus on what you are doing and your purpose for being there.

> *Release your hold on irrational beliefs. Taking small actions toward what you want will help shift your mindset to something more constructive.*

Looking at these scenarios a little more objectively, you might realize a couple of things. First, your distractions, procrastination, or interruption may be a result of misalignment between your values to your desires. To conquer any of these, determine what is most important to you about what you want. Next, your excuses may be habitual and need a shift in mindset and action. Let's say that you have a tendency to surrender to other people's needs and use these noble actions as a reason to prolong or avoid activities you set out to do for yourself. In your mind, you may believe that taking care of others is selfless and a loving gesture. Unfortunately, in your desire to help others, you may find that people continue to put you to work doing exactly what they want and pull you away from your plans. Over time, you succumb to it more and form a habit of being there even when they do not ask for your assistance. As this behavior persists, you may make excuses to be there regardless of whether or not they want your help. In the long run, the feedback you receive from them may not be pleasant or what you expected. Couple that with not achieving your goals, and you might detect an imbalance in your values and priorities. At this juncture, you must prepare your mind through reason to adjust your actions. Your heart may conflict with your head, and making a huge leap could devastate all involved. By taking small steps to manage your internal motivations and external influences, you will gradually develop a more unified approach for yourself and others. Through a conscious choice of what you want to do and small steps to start doing it, you will stop enabling unwanted behavior from yourself and others. The relationship will progress as each will be encouraged to EMBRACE their freedom and practice self-reliance gracefully.

Law of Correspondence - We create patterns that correspond to and enable other patterns in our lives.

The hardest part about doing anything is taking the first step. Through a reasoned mind, you can handle the VENTURE in a more objective view. You become more objective when you drop the excitement, drama, or negativity and make sense out of the situation. Being more objective will naturally allow you to take on a better attitude and begin new activities constructively. With a new outlook, you will feel empowered as you detach yourself from whatever is holding you back and lessen your anxieties about stepping out there.

Jumping In

Ready, set, go! You have done everything you need to set yourself up for success. You have envisioned your big picture, verified it as the direction you want to go, and created goals. Now, you are ready to launch, but alas, you drag your feet. What gives?

Remember, we take risks every day. When you think about your life, doing nothing is <u>still risky</u>. If you choose not to move forward, you face being bored, stagnated, and left behind. How fulfilling, meaningful, and purposeful of a life would that be? On the other hand, if you move forward, regardless of whether you succeed or fail, you experience learning, development, and opportunity in various areas of your life.

Sometimes it is not that you do not want to jump in. You may just not know how to proceed, particularly if a completely new direction or pursuit will impact others or be a lifelong endeavor. When you genuinely believe it will bring out the best in you, you will gain composure. With renewed confidence, you will develop a suitable acceptance of any shortcomings and use them later to increase your learning experience. So, let's move!

Two Left Feet

Most of us VENTURE out there feeling excited but sort of clunky. Sometimes even the simplest things can trip us up. You may feel like you are stumbling over your feet or wandering in circles. It's almost like you have two left feet, or take two steps forward and three steps back. That can be frustrating and disappointing. It's time to stop spinning and take action.

Typically, we feel like we have two left feet when we are not physically, mentally, and emotionally primed. As you begin your VENTURE, maybe you need to place things in plain sight to remind you. Remember to take inventory and do a little research to prepare. Check your level of excitement and your attitude. Before you jump, develop a few supportive actions that will help prepare you to move past old thoughts and feelings that may stop you or push you away.

A new car purchase, for example, is a VENTURE many of us jump into, especially if our old vehicle needs replaced. It can be exciting, yet the process in itself is long and can seem intimidating if you are unprepared. The salespeople are skilled in negotiations and want to sell you the car and everything else they can. If you're trading in your auto, they are going to offer you a price lower than it's worth. You know you will be better off negotiating after you research the trade-in value and the new car's true value, regardless of the sticker price. Along with the research, you'll also want to remain calm, detached, and confident. If you are overly excited or nervous, the salesperson will play on that. When you equip yourself with information and practice maintaining your emotional state, you prepare yourself to make fair trades.

Jumping into any VENTURE can be rather challenging and, at the same time, offer the most incredible self-discoveries. To make how you jump in not feel so awkward, prepare yourself a little to manage options associated with what, who, when, and where. But worry not about stumbling. Remember, when you jump into a new ADVENTURE, the experience will quickly open a whole new perspective and an appreciation of your past, present, and future. After a while, your improved balance and coordination will offer you momentum along with more possibilities and opportunities.

Broaden Horizons

Whenever we start new VENTURES, we end up naturally widening our perspective. Your five senses expand to include the new sights, smells, tastes, touches, and sounds. While this happens, you inevitably form different mental and emotional connections. Over time and with repetition, these connections create a new reality. As you continue with your VENTURE, this process also evolves, and your horizons broaden.

Gaining new experiences and broadening horizons can not only be exciting, but they can also be a little scary. Most of us faced this the first time when we were in school and stood in front of a class and presented something to an audience full of wide-eyed, giggly kids. Not only were we petrified by the spotlight, but we had to remember what to say. As we jumped in, we may have noticed that it wasn't as bad as we once thought. These types of events began our public speaking journey that we can carry with us throughout our lives.

The trick to using this and other experiences to broaden our horizons is to not hold onto fear, and in this case, the fear of criticism. Sadly enough, many of us will lug this fear with us each time we experience a similar event. Until we get a grip on the perceived danger, we will carry a lot of needless anxiety and steer entirely away from those activities. By letting go of unwarranted fears, you'll soon realize these once terrifying experiences will not kill you. As you jump in, they can instead increase your desire to improve and sharpen your skills. You see, your energy behind your fears can be redirected to hone your talents by pushing you to practice a little longer and dig a little deeper for more knowledge. It can kick you out of your comfort zone, generate courage, and help you put your best foot forward. The next time you get in front of people, you'll likely be more knowledgeable, rehearsed, and prepared mentally, emotionally, and physically. By jumping in and facing your fears, you sharpen your skills through your experience and create more opportunities to broaden your horizons even wider. Some of these experiences may even be ones you hadn't previously imagined possible.

> *Law of Vacuum – When you open your mind, you offer more space for thoughts and feelings of prosperity.*

Seize Opportunities

With broadened horizons, you will begin to see endless possibilities. With clarity and focus for what you want to be, do or have, you will know which opportunities to seize. They will be evident and feel intuitive to you. They will generate a sensation in your body that entices you to go after it. If you do not pursue it, you will feel like you are missing out.

As the floodgates of possibilities open, you may find yourself overcome with options. At that point, trust your intuition and jump on the one that you can state out loud without hesitation. The beauty of having many opportunities is that no one selection will be wrong but merely another chance to experience something valuable. When you do not decide and prioritize your choices, you might end up over-analyzing each one, getting stuck in your head, and generating internal conflict. We've all been there. As you sift through them, you will begin to doubt if they are worth your time, effort, and money. The problem is that some opportunities do not show up again as quickly as others. In the end, instead of making confident and quick decisions and actions, your life could end up being a long narrow pipe dream. That is one reason we set goals with progressive timeframes.

What can you do when you get caught in indecision? Look for quick-win options that help you gain momentum. Dr Nobuhiro Hagura, who led the Institute of Cognitive Neuroscience at the University College London team before moving to the National Institute of Communications and Technology in Japan states, "Our brain tricks us into believing the low-hanging fruit really is the ripest. We found that not only does the cost to act influence people's behaviour, but it even changes what we think we see." Because brains are wired to seek out the path of least resistance, intentionally align them with your heart. Any opportunity that makes the process smoother and better aligns with your values will offer the greatest rewards. When you recognize activities that allow you to live your highest values first, you will very likely feel energized and inspired to start right away. As a bonus, you may also have less of a tendency to hold onto what might be perceived as a right or wrong path and quickly recognize what you seek. You'll know what is best because you feel a fullness in your heart, lightness in your head, and butterflies in your stomach. Check for them!

Look, as you VENTURE, if you do not seize opportunities, they will come around again. When they do, jump in! Imagine the opportunities you would miss today if you decided never to take the leap to write your first check, drive for the first time, or apply for your first job. The same goes for the rest of your life. You will be left behind and disappointed with your music still left in you. It is within each of us to take that bold leap and set the stage to seize opportunities and VENTURE into action.

Focus is key

Focus is essential to your development and your entire life. It is critical to include when you want to jump into any VENTURE. As stated earlier, your focus helps you recognize opportunities when you see them. It also enables you to know what to avoid and where to lean on your intuition. Your previous experiences can help you focus by shedding light on what affected you in the past. As you consider these clues and resolve obstacles, you will sharpen your focus, find it easier to decide, and go for it.

#17 focus – where you place your immediate attention offers you clues to your interests, thoughts, and feelings.

Jim Rohn stated it perfectly. Learn to work harder on yourself than you do on your job, or in this case, your external events. But you cannot do this unless you focus on your vision and yourself. Before diving in, you will be best served to know what you want, why you want it, and what it will be like to have it. If you do not, you will tend to revert to the same old things you've been doing. It can be tough to change old habits, especially those you do not readily notice. So, pay attention to how you think and feel, along with what you do.

The magic of focus is that as you move toward your outcome and seize opportunities, other things will seem to disappear. Your brain can only soak in so much information. By not focusing on what you do not want, those parts of your world gradually tend to fade. It's not that they are not there. You simply become aware of them and not fixate on them because you choose to place your attention elsewhere. This idea is like the barking dog or heavy traffic around your neighborhood. After a while, you do not seem to notice it as much, that is, until you place your focus back on it.

Take caution, though. Your ADVENTURE is not the only thing going on in your life. If you jump in and hyperfocus or become too caught up, you may put yourself in danger or find your valuable relationships, things, and events slipping away. As you become more specific, clear, and confident in your vision and how it fits into your life, your decisions become less impulse-driven and more intentional and meaningful.

This happened to me after I won my first bodybuilding contest. I was so excited and hyped about winning. My body was in peak physical condition, and I couldn't wait to take on another contest. I did not realize that I was taxing other parts of my life and my body needed rest. I knew I wanted to compete but struggled to determine how it would all fit with everything else important to me. My intent was to fold in time with my child, work demands, and social activities, but I struggled to juggle it all. Nonetheless, I jumped into my second competition with determination. I struggled to balance competing priorities, a very strenuous diet, an intense workout regimen, and much-needed sleep. I performed well by placing second but knew I was slipping in my regimen. I was not nearly disciplined enough as far as competition prep was concerned. I even tried to use the same diet, exercise, and posing plan as before. Again, I jumped in to compete in the final contest that year. I completely lost focus and placed almost last. I should not have been on the stage. How embarrassing! I also lost valuable time with my child and strained close friendships. My plan certainly didn't work as well as I had hoped. I learned some precious lessons that year. I needed to be clear on all of the outcomes I wanted and VENTURE toward them more sensibly. Although I did so with varying degrees of success, I would have performed better had I waited a while longer before jumping into another competition.

As you focus, you might also want to consider not clinging too tightly to the way others do things. Sometimes when we jump in, we might feel rushed if we believe we are lagging behind or not following some process. Start with the basics and build your unique approach from there. People are not in the same circumstances and do not have the same values, priorities, and passions. Also, realize you bring your DANCE and will have different insights and experiences. As you focus on what you want, your horizon will be unique; thus, your opportunity selection will also. Choose wisely!

The most challenging part about VENTURING into something new is the start. It is uncomfortable and requires change. For some, change is difficult. Normally, it's because we have not EMBRACED where we are right now in our *Zone of Potential*. You may want what others have that you do not. The fact is you will always want, even if you are not sure what that might be. It's natural. Look around. Practically everything up to this point in your life is a product of your needs, wants, and actions. Your past decisions shaped who you are, what you have, and what you do right now. Coincidences are a matter of choice, not chance. Once you choose to recognize this, it will offer you a starting point and possibly a clearer vision of which direction to go. Today is the day you EMBRACE your gifts that led you right to this point in your Zone.

Chapter 5

EMBRACE

When we begin anew, far too often we get caught up in the excitement and desire for immediate gratification. We start too hard, fast, or intense and ignore what is actually happening. Sometimes we generate so much enthusiasm that we may miss or push back on all of the red flags. This happens quite often with 'get-rich-quick' schemes, 'fast-weight-loss' diets, and love at first sight. Sometimes we can experience success in these VENTURES, but quite often, we end up either right back where we began or somewhere else unexpected and undesired. By knowing the details of your vision and EMBRACING your current position, you will tend to release the urge to rush things, better prepare yourself, and be more willing to create and follow a plan.

When we don't EMBRACE our starting point, we struggle to VENTURE and be RESILIENT. This is not just taking inventory. It is accepting where you are and what it will take to get where you want to go. If you do not know where you're starting, your rose-colored, fantasy-laden glasses may frustrate you. Everything has a starting point, that includes relationships, professions, families, homeownership, education, and so on. For whatever reasons, many of us believe these should be smooth, logically structured, and easy to get. In some rare cases, that may seem true. For others, life is filled with many challenges. Franklin Delano Roosevelt understood this and described it well through this pithy statement, "A smooth sea never made a skilled sailor." The sailor certainly did not start as an expert. Don't place that pressure on yourself to think you will either.

Keep in mind that you have plenty of gifts to help you pave your way. These gifts were given to you or created by you in your past and currently exist in your life. It is time to examine your gifts and determine how they can support you. Remember, your perception is your reality. See the gift and opportunity in what you have, and you will be able to design your life the way you want it.

Looking Back

Everyone has a past. We all know this. And, whether we like it or not, we also lug it around with us everywhere we go. It can be a sack of dirty laundry or a basket of goodies. In the end, with careful contemplation, you will notice that these containers are filled with gifts of opportunity for you to learn and grow.

Most of us know that everything happens for a reason. The problem is, we cannot seem to grasp the reason, especially while we are going through it. We may get stuck in denial and the feelings of regret, shame, guilt, sadness, and a host of negative emotions. While in low spirits, you may even be tempted to cling to things, people, and activities that help you soothe your emotional states. As time goes on, we can get trapped deeper in our old ways and stifle our ability to ENJOY even the thought of experiencing something new. You will gain a more balanced perspective of life's lessons, however, when you view both positive and negative past events as gifts. Through a balanced lens, you become more objective and less preoccupied with where you are now.

My youngest brother took a balanced perspective in how life unfolded for him. Alex was a bit of a surprise, with the youngest of his six other siblings being nine years older than him. That was a huge gap with 14 years total to reach the eldest. As Alex was growing up, he said it was like being an only child. Even the schools considered him a single child as none of the teachers knew his brothers and sisters from many years before. Alex said that by the time he left high school, he was just starting to have the ability to recall aspects about his elder siblings. The next thing he knew, I was in the Marine Corps, and he was the only child left in the house as he headed into middle school.

When I asked Alex how he felt his upbringing was different from the older kids, he said life was easy. Alex participated in many activities and received things that the other children did not because, back then, our parents could not afford the same for so many of us. We both guessed that Mom and Dad were making up for lost time and their inability to provide personal attention to all six children at once. Although he had friends and loved going to the movies, playing video games, and reading books, Alex also had to learn to entertain himself when he was home alone.

Unlike the older group of six, Alex said he felt like he had everything he needed. As such, he did not feel compelled to drive so hard and knew intuitively that, in time, he would receive everything he needed. Alex had little worries and developed a calm, relaxed personality. He also learned to appreciate the balanced perspective between being part of a large family and his personal space. Alex's biggest realization about how he was raised was that you can be part of a big family and still be treated and feel like an only child. Although Alex did not have to compete for attention from our parents or deal with sibling rivalry, he could have felt left out and alone. Instead, he took a balanced approached, EMBRACED what he learned, and, to this day, applies that same principle with his wife and two children as a loving, caring, compassionate husband and father.

The events of your life are all based on your focus, decisions, actions, energy, and so on. You are only the sum of your past experiences if that is what you choose. Simply put, they are just the result of who you have been and what you have been doing. These are your gifts of learning, and you will continue to create and use them. Finding your gifts will bring you back into balance, where you live authentically, objectively, and with reason. By EMBRACING these gifts, you can truly learn to love life.

Law of Balance and Harmony – Everything strives to be in perfect balance. Life will balance itself back into alignment from cause & effect and positive & negative experiences to obtain harmony.

Your Past in Action

No matter how you look at it, your environment has had the most significant impact on who you've become today. In every aspect of your life, you've witnessed and experienced many events that shaped how you look at the world. Your background includes everything from where you have lived, your social circles, your workplace, and everything else in between. These factors influenced your decisions and choices based on what attracted or repulsed you. Sometimes you ENJOYED the outcome, and other times not so much. For the most part, your memories posed as a baseline to make similar decisions and transform your identity and life.

So, how do you become a product of your environment? As children, our neighborhoods, cultures, communities, classrooms, playgrounds, etc., stood as learning environments and a baseline for determining what we want. In each place, you encountered people, things, and events. You incorporated ideas, beliefs, and concepts from your interactions to support what you accepted or rejected. These influenced your focus and continued to change as you grew. In effect, you formed your own unique way of viewing the world. This, in turn, led to your development and refinement of habits, routines, and rituals you may still use today.

Let's just take a quick look at the people in your earlier years. Your parents, guardians, and close family members are usually the first to influence your life. They did more than give you love, food, and shelter. They told you and showed you how to live based on what they knew or what worked for them. You were subject to their values, and you did your best to decide which ones will work for you. As it so happened with me, Dad influenced me most in my professional areas. Mom's influence mainly came in my interpersonal relationships. I saw their lessons as baselines and, to this day, weigh the pros and cons to pick what works best at any given time. It does not always turn out the way I want, but at least I have modeled behavior from which to choose. You very likely have the same based on what your parental figures demonstrated.

Your siblings and friends also taught you how to be social and helped create your identity. Together, you watched, listened, and learned how to interact, have fun, and care for each other. Friendships gradually expanded, contracted, and evolved as your life changed. On the other hand, rivals provided opportunities for you to learn RESILIENCE, develop coping skills, and build moral courage. Many other people directly or indirectly taught you and helped you develop into who you are today.

Although it may sound simple, it's not. Your environment is very complex and can also create challenges when you do not let go of what is no longer helpful. You have to let go of what you think you know to get where you want to go. Over time, we may hold onto judgments about who we would have been, what we should think and feel, and how we should act. These can become so hardwired and difficult to change that you may end up frustrated and anxious. There's a gift in simply recognizing our thoughts, feelings, and actions. With recognition, we now have the power to choose what to keep that works and ditch what does not.

Law of New Beginnings – Any major life turning point will change your direction.

There is so much more to our environment than what is on the surface. All of this is a part of who you are, so choosing what you want from your surroundings would make sense. Also, if where you are does not offer you the opportunity to experience what you want, you can change your location until you find it. Do you want to carry all this baggage and conceal your unique qualities? For the most part, you cannot change everything around you. But you can change where you are, how you are thinking and feeling, and what you are doing.

Lessons in Clutter

Our surroundings are filled with stuff we've accumulated over the years. We have certain objects that reflect what we love doing and simplify our lives. As you recall all of the things you had and now have, you might notice that it reflects what you valued and what brought you joy. Just like the people in your life, this stuff changes over time.

As you transitioned from childhood to adult life, your leisure objects, such as toys, games, sports equipment, books, tools, etc., shifted with you. You went from simple toys to more complex, thought-provoking ones. Your career and family life added to your collection of stuff to include work clothes, play clothes, tools, gadgets, books, equipment, trinkets, and even bigger toys, like real cars, trucks, boats, and planes. Collecting continues on into retirement and through to your end of life. No matter where you are in life, you can see reflections of how your past contributed to your learning and where you are today.

Although the items of your past offer valuable memories, they also have some drawbacks. One major challenge is that we hold onto our stuff and constantly relive the memories like time stood still. We lug our old clothing, equipment, and other items with us like we are going to use them again. We may even put them in boxes or display them to relive the experiences. There's nothing really wrong with that unless they interfere with your desire to move beyond your past. When your life changes, so will the value you place on your stuff. The more you add, the more you increase your responsibility to store and maintain it. The resulting clutter can overwhelm your thoughts and feelings of obtaining something new for the future and can keep you attached to the past.

As you look around at your stuff, you may notice what's keeping you in yesteryear. It's time to EMBRACE the past as just that, the past. You can bring some nostalgic items with you or take photos of them as fond memories, but let the rest go. It will shed you of the old and make room for what's important to you now and what is yet to come.

Our belongings can offer us so many gifts of information about ourselves. The things you own give insight into who you've been. When you EMBRACE the items of your past, you can use that as a starting point to effect change. In DANCE, you inventoried what you have to start. Here, you EMBRACE the stuff of your past so you can realize where you've been and make intentional choices for the future. The environment and clutter are only part of the battle. They're much easier to notice because you can see them outside of you. EMBRACING the gifts of information on the inside of your emotional backpack is where the real fun begins.

> *Law of Summarized Experiences – You are the sum total of everything that has happened to you.*

Emotional Backpack

Since birth, we have been on a learning trek to figure out how to get what we want out of life. As babies, before we could speak, we naturally cried in distress to be fed, changed, and held. Sometimes we threw fits of anger to get whatever we wanted. We learned how frustrating we can become when we do not know how to express ourselves through words. We also learned how laughter, joy, and generosity affected others. As our verbal skills improved and communications skills evolved, we

#5 conception – we are all born as pure love, then life on Earth happens. Do your best to master its complexities. See them for what they are and know you are above it all!

started to ask more clearly for what we wanted. This feeling and thought learning cycle continued throughout our lives and have since become habits based on our comfort levels and what worked.

Here's the deal. Every decision you make has an attached emotion. Every step you made in the past started with an idea, caused a sense of desire, created rationalized thoughts, and ended with another feeling. You are where you are today because you felt comfortable, confident, safe, or some other affirming emotion in your decisions. By EMBRACING this notion, you will begin to understand how your and everyone else's feelings are both natural and valid.

We must face our feelings because they are gifts that tell us where we begin emotionally. Even if we turn away from them, rest assured they will still be there. By the time you are an adult, you will have experienced every emotion that exists, every one! Your long-held emotions are the ones that affect every aspect of your life. Some people call these your shadow side. You cannot see them, and rarely do you know the extent of which they guide your actions.

Once you become AWAKE to your emotions, you will see how they have supported or sabotaged your progress. But you must first EMBRACE that they exist. Simply realizing this reality is hard work and takes practice for many of us, but the rewards are truly magical. To make the process easier, approach it with self-love. Work is easier with love and becomes harder when performed without it. As you grow into this realization, you will develop the ability to consciously EMBRACE the gifts in your feelings and notice how you best used them to you get what you want. Otherwise, you will relinquish your personal power, get whatever feedback that shows up, and stay stuck in your muck.

Stuck in the Muck

With all the richness you experienced in your past, one would think it would be a wonderful recollection of memories. For some, that may be evident. For others, maybe they just haven't taken the time to recognize and appreciate them. I bet you have tackled many amazing feats. You've

Reflect on your past and EMBRACE the truth about how you created your life. Doing so allows you to knock down old barriers holding you back from new experiences and a meaningful life.

91

overcome demanding jobs, troubled relationships, challenges with health, money matters, etc. Even if you lived in survival mode, you learned and created solutions that worked. Many of us seldom recognize these as achievements because when we use them again in other situations, they do not seem to work as well. As times change, so too must our solutions.

As noted earlier, our emotional tactics began at childhood and developed roots through adolescence into adulthood. Children will physically throw fits to get what they want until the outbursts no longer work. They then start scheming in other ways. By the time they reach their teens, they have concocted various strategies to get what they want. Then comes adulthood. As adults, we drag these tactics into other areas of our lives and use them to satisfy our needs as long as they work. If unsuccessful, we may modify them or try something different. After enough trial and error, we become frustrated and sometimes blame our external circumstances. This is when we get stuck in our muck. Change must come from each of us first!

Our muck is like mud. Most of us are doing our best not to drag that muck along in our backpacks. If you insist on lugging it around, you will make a mess all over. And, the more unpleasant it gets, the more it can become

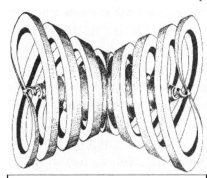

#8 gyres – our thought and feeling patterns create whirling, spiral, and circular motions that keeps us in the same eternal loops. Eventually, they can pick up speed and keep us stuck in a state of endless desires for things we never receive.

like quicksand where you suffocate as you strain in it. There's a better way. Stop for a moment to EMBRACE and face your past with awe and fascination. The gifts are in the baseline that inform you of how you repetitively think, feel, and act today. The longer you ignore your old patterns, the more you will struggle to use what works. What remains are the effects of your unproductive, disruptive, and destructive ways. Your life, along with the people and circumstances in it, is in a constant state of change. As you EMBRACE your past, you can use these gifts to create something different and flow with everything around you. Every aspect of your life contains gifts that are waiting for you to open. It is up to you to find them and choose which will work.

Life's Wonderful Gifts

Life in and of itself is a beautiful gift. The mere fact that the degree to which we can intentionally choose what we want is beyond what any other species can do. That does not mean life was ever meant to be easy. Your many circumstances and opportunities can be pleasant surprises or painful hardships. All of us have been given particular challenges to guide us in our individual growth and development. Whether you receive them unexpectedly or create them yourself, they all offer something unique. If you ignore them, you miss out on learning all they offer. These are your individual gifts from which you learn, create, teach, and master.

Luck of the Draw

With every decision we carry out, we receive a gift of feedback. This exchange is the law of cause and effect. For every action, there's an equal and opposite reaction. Some may consider this good luck and bad luck, but really, it's the cause of being somewhere or doing something at certain times. Earl Nightingale once said, "Luck is when preparedness meets opportunity." For example, you would not have won the lottery if you didn't get a ticket before the draw. You also would not have lost all of it if you knew what to do with it once you had it. Those are simple illustrations, but our lives are quite similar.

Law of Cause and Effect (Karma) - Every cause has an effect; every effect is a result of a cause. Be the cause to achieve the effect desired for you and all. You will receive back the same positive and negative thoughts and actions you give.

The more you are prepared and armed with knowledge about yourself and any situation, the more you will be apt to encounter perceived good luck. The same is true for your past. Had you not made the many decisions to be who and where you were when you did, you would not have had the same experiences. As you look at your past, you'll begin to notice how the effects of your decisions shaped your success. Your actions led to plenty of positive outcomes, including opportunities that simply showed up. Think about it. Intuition, timing, and positive energy used together can help you score the most convenient parking spot, easy traffic, and perfect weather on a day you planned something special. Although it could feel a lot like luck, the gift is based on your decisions about where you are, what you focus on, and your actions. It doesn't matter if you use reason, intuition, or guesswork. What was supposed to happen, happened. Ultimately, each one of us creates our results and our fortunes.

What about bad luck? Luck is luck. It comes about the same way. Just like good luck, we experience bad luck through our actions, emotions, and energy that, in this case, create undesirable results. We have all had bouts of unfortunate situations where things didn't go our way, or we missed out on opportunities. These misfortunes also exist as gifts to guide you in your personal development by letting you know what does not work and where

you are placing your attention. These clues tell us to adjust our energy and be more prepared. Have you ever noticed when you are prepared, nothing really bothers you? Have you ever noticed when you search too hard and become stressed, you cannot find what you're looking for? Have you ever noticed when you relax and know what you want, it seems to show up? When you are truly ready for something, it will happen for you. Otherwise, you will be on a learning path until you are ready for it. EMBRACE where you are and what you have so you can relax and recognize opportunities as they show up!

#28 lucy locket – a carefree feeling is like a happy, breezy day. Preparedness helps you be ready for anything. Mix the two and watch prosperity unfold!

As you EMBRACE the gifts you have created for yourself, you will begin to see that you are in the driver's seat. You will start to feel more confident, secure, and at ease knowing there is a reason for everything that happens. Your good luck charms can then become anchors to remind you to be prepared, focus on what you want, and take advantage of opportunities. What you consider bad luck, Murphy's Law, and other omens can be used as an awareness for you to proceed with caution, learn, and adjust for the future. Along the way, you will be better prepared for other gifts you might receive that simply show up.

Curve Balls

Beyond the events we bring on ourselves, curve balls are the ones that we did not ask to receive and just show up, uninvited, out of nowhere. It seems as though life has a way of handing us curve balls that pull us away from or add to our already challenging lives. Sometimes these can last a whole lifetime.

Curve balls are also the ones that you don't directly own but feel compelled to insert yourself because you are a part of or responsible for them. Something about these curve balls tug on your heartstrings. We all have examples of these in our lives. As you work through the challenges they present, at some point you will likely discover the 'gifts' in them, too. An example of this is when a baby is born with a disability or a parent, child, or sibling unexpectedly becomes critically ill. Although they didn't choose the illness nor the impact it has on others, it exists. Depending on the severity, it can create a whole host of challenges for family and friends.

Most people question why they fell victim to these burdens, regardless if they are the person with the disability or the caregiver who abruptly alters their lives to tend to the other's needs. Yet each person can uncover the gift if they so choose. These unique circumstances and people can offer us opportunities to reflect and discover a more profound sense of patience, compassion, and love in ourselves, even if we are indirectly involved.

Mother Nature's events can also throw us curve balls. Natural disasters can leave a damaging impact on us. You can be aware of many disasters as they ramp up, like hurricane warnings, flooding, and even sometimes tornado alerts. Yet sometimes, they can be unpredictable, like an earthquake or a random tornado. Not very many people in the Washington, D.C. area realized they were on an active fault line when an earthquake happened in August 2011. Mike, my good friend and fellow Marine, never expected a tornado to come ripping through his town and flattening his house. He certainly wasn't in tornado alley. Once again, you would not want to wish the disastrous effects on anyone, but they can happen in any one of our lives. For each of us, these circumstances offer us a chance to reflect on what is most important, including as an outsider lending a hand in support. In these types of situations, you can experience a variety of gifts, such as RESILIENCE, community, and graciousness.

Most people certainly do not look at any of these events as gifts, especially when they are the ones devastated. We would more so expect negative feelings of being stuck, helpless, or lost. Mike wasn't going to have any of that as he gathered up his belongings from the neighborhood. One surefire way to get beyond those feelings is to EMBRACE that it happened, and know that you cannot change it. When you allow yourself to do so, you'll then create a more neutral perspective so you can pull out the positive side, the gift. Mike did just that. He knew what was most important, like his dog Dexter, and other valuables. With homeowner insurance in tow, he knew he was starting over with a clean slate. Because of his positive attitude, people lovingly open their arms to help him clean up, and businesses offered him professional services for a substantially reduced rate. Although nothing replaced the devastation, he was able to extract gifts in the disaster, even beyond physical. Every situation has an advantage. When you discover the gift, you can reason better and handle events less emotionally and more creatively. The final decision lies entirely with you to realize the gift and what to do with it.

We are all given a host of circumstances to help us learn, create, teach, and ultimately master our lives. Once you figure out the gift in one area, another opportunity will arise. That gift will depend on what you need to learn next. EMBRACE these events, uncover the gifts they offer, and use them to make life your favorite ADVENTURE. In doing so, you not only create solutions for yourself but have the knowledge to help and share with others experiencing the same.

Law of Faith - Know without fear that what happens is supposed to happen, regardless of what it is.

Wake-Up Calls

One of the major traits we carry around is our individual disabilities we are born with or acquired. These, like the curve balls mentioned above, are what we learn to build our lives around so we can survive and thrive. The funny thing is, even though you may have had these disabilities all of your life or for an extended period, you probably never really considered them a gift or valuable. Many of us often see them as roadblocks to our success. If you think about it for a moment, it is not your disability that holds you back. It is your attitude about it. Our disabilities only get in our way if we allow them. Their purpose is to lead us on our paths to something greater than where we are. For some people, their disabilities motivate them to try something challenging that many others are unwilling to do. They see their disabilities as another facet of themselves that makes their life unique!

As a young boy, my husband delivered newspapers with one of his closest friends, Darren. Darren had so many things going for him. He was an amazing multi-sport athlete in high school, very intelligent, and had several career prospects ahead of him. When Darren was in his 20s, the doctor told him they would need to operate on a portion of his brain that had a 50-50 chance of retaining his eyesight, or he'd go blind. Darren took that chance, and life as he knew it came to a screeching halt. He landed on the 50 percent blind. As you can imagine, he was very distraught. Almost everything about his life had to change. Darren knew he had a long road ahead to learn how to live independently with his blindness. For the next couple of years, he learned how to read through touch, navigate his world beyond his sense of sight, and rely on others for help. He married a lovely lady, and they began a new life together. Although he was not pleased with his disability, he soon found opportunities in it, especially in the areas of technical accessibility. As technology was quickly advancing, developers failed to consider the various physical disabilities. Darren stepped up to the challenge and began helping big tech companies design and test accessibility programs and applications. He stood out by helping create technical solutions so people dealing with blindness could live more independent lives. He committed his purpose to bring value into the world and help others through his circumstances. While he surely didn't ask for it, and society may have seen his blindness as devastation, Darren treated it as a gift to transform the lives of others living with the same disability.

Most disabilities make us stand out. And, if you recognize that it is only one aspect of your life, you will be able to EMBRACE the gift in it and utilize it to help serve others. We've already mentioned Stephen Hawking, Sammy Davis Jr., and Helen Keller. But this goes beyond physical. Many famous people have emotional and mental disabilities, such as Asperger's, dyslexia, schizophrenia, Tourette's, and the list goes on. Some may have sought help for a cure, and others learned how to deal with them and overcome the power they can hold. None of us have to like living with a disability, but we can EMBRACE that it is something in our *Zone of Potential* to master. As a side note, just because you admit you have a disability does not mean you have to accept all of your old assumptions and beliefs about it. You are unique with a rich, resourceful past that led you to where you are today. This is your wake-up call. EMBRACE it! We all grapple with finding solutions to overcome our inability to function in certain areas of our lives. Start questioning your current assumptions and beliefs of the past to create your desired future.

Presents in Presence

You are living the sum of your many remarkable decisions, and everything that surrounds you reflects that. This is your beautiful design, and you fit it perfectly. It is all you, and you have the right to be proud of your creation. You are responsible for every bit of it. Take a moment and notice where you are, what you have become, and what is going on in your life.

For many of us, life is grand! For others, not so much. Many people have not moved on from their past or are constantly concerned about their future. They live with regrets, guilt, shame or worry, fear, and anxiety. The fact is, the past is gone, and we cannot change that. The future has not even arrived yet, so it can be consciously designed however you desire. It is a mystery waiting to unfold. The only thing you truly have is now, the present. EMBRACE it and stay in the moment so you can prepare for what's to come.

Be With Me, Here

Many of us have heard that we should be present with ourselves, others, and surroundings. Being constantly self-aware and paying attention to everything around you is virtually impossible and can be pretty tricky. Your mind is constantly busy, even while you sleep. Your memories of the past or self-generated stories of what will happen in the future come up all of the time. You cannot stop them, and they can get in your way of being in the moment. This is very distracting and can create problems, especially when you need to focus.

When we are not present, we become forgetful, do mindless unimportant things, and feel detached from everything. How many times have you walked into a room without a clue as to why you were there? What about the excessive amount of food, drink, cigarette, or social media we consume without realizing we are doing it? We ignore conversations, do not see details around us, and rarely take the time to notice when things are off. It's almost like we are not in our bodies.

Being in the moment will loosen your grip on regrets and worry and help you become more focused and intentional. You will begin to notice things about your partner, children, siblings, friends, and so on, that you have missed. When you eat, you will not only better notice the taste and texture, but you will also know when you begin to feel satisfied. Your mindfulness will help you detect triggers for behaviors that you want to avoid. All of these and more are useful in living a fulfilling life. You will feel happier and more appreciative of what you have and what you've done. You will be more honest with yourself and have more confidence and energy to make better decisions. You will experience peace and calmness in the circumstances you cannot change. This can be incredibly freeing. As a result, you will improve your relationships with everything and everyone in your environment, but most importantly, with yourself. Although distractions and intrusions will still occur, with improved presence, you will recognize them for what they are in each situation and handle them with dignity and grace.

Interruptions Interrupted

Stop bugging me! Researchers at the University of California, Irvine, found that workers are interrupted every 11 minutes. On top of that, it took 25 minutes for them to become refocused on their work. We all know that interruptions come into our world and disrupt our train of thought and concentration. We allow them to get between us, our present moment, and our activities. Although we often create strategies to tackle them, how we manage ourselves during these interruptions can make all the difference.

Your quick willingness to give in to unnecessary interruptions can indicate whether your head and heart are in the game. Something also may be going on that requires your attention for you to become present again. It could be competing priorities and values, or maybe you simply do not ENJOY what you are doing. Perhaps you're seeking immediate pleasure and gratification elsewhere, or maybe it's something else. Whatever it is, this is your opportunity to figure it out, EMBRACE it, and choose what to do with these situations in the future. Glossing over them will only pull you from your present moment, create frustrations, and entice you to develop unhelpful habits. The last thing you want is for these interruptions to become distractions that keep you from achieving your goals. Here is where setting time-bound goals becomes so important. They can help you prioritize activities and keep you on track. Otherwise, the interruptions will increase, everything else will take precedence, and you may never achieve your goal.

Distraction Destroyers

Whereas interruptions are external disruptions we allow into our moments, distractions are the decisions we make to divert our attention. Interruptions cause distractions, but we are often distracted by other things than mere interruptions. Harvard psychologists conducted a study that suggests our minds wander about 47% of our waking hours, and most of us don't even realize it when it's happening. How is it that every time we get into the groove, we can easily slip out of it, become forgetful, and start thinking of or doing other things? You are surrounded by objects, people, and events that do not interrupt you until you shift your focus to and are triggered by them. Prime examples of this are our cell phones and email inboxes. These are the biggest distractions in today's society. For many of us, these tools stay by our side so we can stay connected and get work done.

Here's how it works. Of all the data around us, we each pick and choose where we place our focus. These bright shiny objects of distraction seem to draw us toward them and detract us from being present and in the moment. Everything else within view and earshot is deleted, blurred, or ignored. This point tells us that we pay attention to whatever we want. This, just like our disruptions, is also a part of life. If we EMBRACE that these distractions exist, we can then develop strategies to help us refocus our thoughts, feelings, and actions to keep or get us back on track. Both interruptions and distractions can tend to be exhausting and discouraging. Again, it's not about accepting or surrendering to them. It is merely EMBRACING the likelihood of them so you can control your reactions to them. Otherwise, if you succumb to them, they may become habitual. These new habits may begin to feel like you are being productive and multitasking. The truth is, by scattering your focus, you miss out on opportunities to give any of these activities the full attention they deserve.

Multitasking Myth

Many of us over-achievers and high-producers love to think we are multitasking. It gives us a sense that we are accomplishing so much at one time. But is this true? In reality, multitasking is a process where we rapidly switch from one task to another. The sequencing can be all over the place or well-structured, but ultimately, we are only really doing one thing at a time, just with less individualized attention. That's how our brains are wired.

As you can imagine, because our attention is so divided when we multitask, we tend to make mistakes. You see, we need time to fully reorient back into a previous task or we become much less efficient. We may even endanger ourselves and others. This is the primary reason we have laws to keep us from using our cell phones while driving, especially texting. We have enough to tend to inside and outside of the vehicle. By spreading our attention more broadly, we increase the risks of having accidents.

Invariably, we will continue to juggle tasks. It's how we enhance our flexibility and adaptability to increase our RESILIENCE. Multitasking allows us to operate in complexity, such as driving cars, listening to music while exercising, and preparing multiple similar orders. Where we fall short is when we need to focus. Multitasking scatters your attention and strips you of the ability to concentrate on one thing. As you bounce from one activity to another, you may find it tough to think and forget what you were doing. You might feel like you're in chaos. If multitasking becomes habitual, you will start to notice declines in quality, completion, and social skills. The resulting effects could lead to burnout as you become overwhelmed with various thoughts and activities. It's a disaster waiting to happen. To get past this struggle, recognize when it's happening

> *Pause, prioritize, and place your full attention on who and what you value most.*

and pause for a moment. Place priorities on each task according to its value and time. If something is important enough, we typically proceed with great care. It isn't just busyness; this means business! If done correctly, you will get as much done as you can during that time and eventually see it through to completion. When you become organized with your priorities, you will feel more confident about the accuracy of your outcome. Not only that, you will feel accomplished and satisfied when you complete more of what you value. If you don't organize your day, everything and everyone else will do it for you. Choose and arrange by priority what's most important.

As you EMBRACE your desire to do many things, serve many people, and leave a lasting impression, you will soon figure out where multitasking has its place in your life. It certainly would be beneficial to avoid when doing dangerous activities and those that bring great value or joy. Slow your roll, concentrate on your top priorities, be in the moment with what matters the most, and experience a life you can appreciate and ENJOY. Again, it is all up to you. You are the interior designer of your life, so create it how you want it!

Gift of Interior Design

Once we recognize how our past becomes our present and affects our future, we have more power to choose wisely. If you want the same thing, stick with what has worked while it still works. If you want something different or more out of life, you must pay attention to what your present situation is telling you. In this way, you'll be able to take actions that create lesson-rich memories for a future you love and become your own interior life designer! As designers, we make what we want with intention, flow, and determination. As stated in VENTURE, none of this comes without taking risks. To generate the confidence that you are going in the right direction, you need a level of certainty, faith in yourself, and small wins. One way to do that is to empty out your backpack, keep what works, and ditch what does not. With the space you create, you can then fill your bucket with proven tools along with your newly discovered ones and use them for any of your next ADVENTURES.

Law of Release - Let go of anything no longer useful and purposeful without regret and resentment.

Empty Your Backpack

In VENTURE, we talked about cleaning out our closets. As with any interior designer, you will benefit most from knowing what you have from the start. Unless you take this into account, your design might not capture your uniqueness, and you won't have a clear idea of what to do first. It can be quite frustrating and exhausting trying to create something that doesn't suit you and your style. By emptying your backpack, you will have a better idea of what to keep and ditch.

Earlier in this chapter, we EMBRACED our clutter and our emotional backpacks as a part of our past and present. Now is the time to dump it all out, assess the gifts of your past, and sort them out for what you want next. Initially, you may feel overwhelmed when you dump everything out. Your backpack has more than just a few years; it has a lifetime. It can be like hauling a mountain of school books that get heavy and weigh you down over time. Strangely enough, even with a high volume of knowledge and wisdom, we gravitate toward the same books and wear them out. Undoubtedly, they are what guided us in the past to make the same choices. Yet even when they don't work for us anymore, we still hold tightly to them. If your gifts no longer deliver what you want, you must be willing to toss them aside. As you do, save the gifts still serving you and EMBRACE fresh ideas for new gifts to come. Your books are specially designed for your learning. You just need to choose the ones that work best for what you want next.

Your volumes of knowledge and wisdom include information about emotional attachments, assigned meanings, and physical objects, among other exciting details. Emotional attachments are those feelings you get when you see, hear, touch, taste, and smell something. They are easily detectable through your attitude and how you react. For example, your current emotional attachment to money will keep you financially where you are unless you change your feelings about it. If the sight of someone else having a large amount of it gives you feelings of low self-worth or jealousy, those feelings may either kick you into gear to go after it or keep you complaining at a distance. The same goes for assigning meaning. If you describe money as the root of all evil or a burden of responsibility, you will struggle to see the good its energy can do for you and others. Finally, as physical objects, your fixation on accumulating money might generate financial wealth, but it does not mean you will experience a wealth of happiness, love, or joy. Your attachment to objects can create triggers that hold you back. It's time to pull them out of your backpack, imagine a greater ability with them or a life without them, and EMBRACE new gifts of prosperity.

Law of Relativity - Nothing makes a difference in this universe until you assign meaning to it and bring into your reality.

By emptying and questioning each item in your backpack, you will gain more simplicity in what you want to design with what you choose to keep. This process may take a while, but the clarity you gain is well worth it. In the process, you will uncover even more aspects about yourself. Grab hold of all of your insights, fill your bucket with them, and save space for new ones because the ADVENTURE of self-discovery has just begun.

Fill Your Bucket

We all have an abundance of gifts to fill our buckets. You carry knowledge and ideas, every feeling to be felt, and your unique talents and skills. These gifts are your personal effects that can be applied to your life. As you unpacked your backpack, you may have found that not every gift continues to give, so let's EMBRACE the ones that will and prepare to put them to work.

As you begin to fill your bucket, consider whether you are comparing the gifts in your bucket to someone else's. If you believe someone else's bucket is running over, you may doubt if what you have will work. This is natural and neither good nor bad. Here is where you EMBRACE curiosity and eliminate doubt by confirming what you need and consciously choosing what works for you. Remember, people are on their own paths and carry their own buckets filled with gifts from their past and in the present to live their purpose. EMBRACE the differences and compare only to decide what you want to design, not to judge.

Tied to our comparisons is our perceptions of right and wrong. Your bucket must be filled and used your way, even if it's the long way or a shortcut. Any design you choose will inevitably include opportunities to learn and create. Remember, we live in a world of infinite possibilities. There is no one specific way to do things. How you think, what you think, and why you think the thoughts you do make your life unique to you. Your thought processes may point you in a completely different direction, and for whatever reason, that is very likely the best direction for you to learn. When you leave your right/wrong perceptions out of the bucket, you will discover more flexibility, creativity, and opportunities to design a life you ENJOY.

Another comparison we make is in our abilities. Let's face it. Someone out there will be smarter, faster, bigger, calmer, more energized, etc., than you are. EMBRACE it! When you put others on high pedestals, you undermine your thoughts about performing at the same level. On the flip side, when you consistently believe your performance is superior to them, you may restrict further development. We all have certain abilities in which we excel. Once again, use these comparisons only to determine how you want to design your life, not to judge. If certain people are very advanced, bring them and their knowledge into your ADVENTURE and develop your skills.

The best part about all of this is that nearly everything you want to know and put in your bucket is at your fingertips. As your bucket begins to fill, you may find that you are thirsty for more. Fill it with as much knowledge as you can. Although it can be wonderful to learn, in the same breath, it can also create a lot of anxiety if you are not sure which direction to go next. By EMBRACING that you are perfectly

> ⚡ *Use technology to quickly research new and existing ways to design your unique life.*

where you need to be, you will soon appreciate the creator in you and start seeing opportunities to design an exceptional life. Be curious like a child. Whatever you are missing will eventually appear if you stay focused and invest in yourself over the long haul.

Invest in Your Development

Keep in mind you are the most important part of your life. Invest time in yourself. Without you, you wouldn't be having any ADVENTURE. We all have personal areas of growth potential. It starts on the inside and can be observed through our actions. As interior designers, you owe it to yourself to enhance your outer experiences through inner work. Carve out space on your calendar to study and reflect on your thoughts and feelings. This is where opportunity awaits. You have the wisdom within, and you know what's standing in your way. You can also lean on others to help reveal your roadblocks. As you contemplate the answers, you will find it easier to identify and deliberately choose to avoid options that stand in the way of your design. Make an effort to understand yourself better, and you will soon be armed with inner tools to design your outer world.

As you candidly evaluate where you are and how you arrived, you may naturally feel a bit nervous about your design and what you are preparing to do. Just remember, all things happen for a reason and at a time that is right for you. You'll know whether the strategy and pace are optimal by the amount of chaos or stress they generate, but keep in mind both are necessary to grow. The greatest successes were achieved through the most significant challenges. So, get to know the size and scope of what is in your way and your willingness to tackle it.

> *Law of Divine Order – Thoughts, words, emotions, and deeds create your environment at the appropriate time for you and not by accident.*

Let Go to Grow

A new VENTURE can often begin with a very optimistic start, perhaps even overly optimistic. Instead of EMBRACING the present, we might be too worried about tomorrow. Sometimes we find things happen too fast, too slow, or maybe there is too much or too little. This polarization can become disruptive unless we see the gift in each side. These "too this" or "too that" are clues telling us to pay attention. Our timing may be off, or maybe we are forcing what has yet to evolve to the right level. Things happen when they are meant to. Don't let worries stop you from taking action. Haste makes waste! Recognize the learning opportunity in it and practice patience as you watch surprises show up. Each surprise is a chance to experience something new and increase your self-development. When you decide to EMBRACE these as gifts, you learn to release the painful desires of immediate gratification. You will also push away from the feeling of being needy and other negative influences. As my sister Heidi would say, "If you think you should be starting at the top, remember, there's only one way to go from there – down." She is a prime example of how steady, challenging work will get you to the top.

From hands-on garage mechanic to VP of a multimillion-dollar oilfield, marine, and industrial clutch company, everything Heidi accomplished opened doors for more opportunity and prosperity. At the young age of 17, Heidi started working in a garage as a car mechanic. She knew what hard work meant and ENJOYED every bit of the mechanical field. Although her focus was on doing whatever she could to ensure her children were cared for, Heidi always had a job and gave 100% to each one. She also knew success didn't happen overnight and did not skip steps or allow challenges to push her away.

Gifted and dependable, new and recurring customers alike ENJOYED Heidi's ability to get exactly what they wanted on time, every time. Little did she know her life-long hard work and generosity were going to pay off. As Heidi demonstrated her organized, efficient, and knowledgeable DANCE in her line of work, management took note. She quickly moved to office manager and soon after became VP of the company. Heidi stayed steady and true to her values and paved her way forward. As she looked back, Heidi realized she could accomplish anything when she put her mind to it. Life isn't always predictable. With steady focus and a pace that offers growth and professional development, you will soon see your design come to life as opportunities come your way.

Another thing to consider as interior designers is your tendency to be so rigid with yourself and the outcome. Sometimes we expect our results to be exactly like we expected or what others experienced. This is unrealistic as all situations are different for each of us. You bring your uniqueness and could drive yourself crazy if you expect your experiences to be perfect or identical to others. To design something unique, you must be willing to develop yourself as a leader and master of your internal world that shapes your life. To lead means to stand in front, and to master means to have control over. So, as you stand in front and control your actions, use your personal power to design what resonates with you and not force your desires to the forefront. The fact is, your pace, DANCE, tools, and energy, along with your internal thought processes, all play into your design. That is how you manage expectations, stay flexible, and let go to grow.

Finally, while designing your future, be aware of your desire to compete with others. We all compete; EMBRACE it! Most of us want to have the best of the best in our lives. But that doesn't necessarily mean we are willing to take on responsibilities associated with the best of the best. Our responsibilities go beyond ourselves and include the impact we have on our surroundings. If your competitive desires are so strong, you may leave a path of destruction behind you. We both know this has the tendency to shut down valuable relationships and potential partnerships that could have strengthened your design along the way. An overly competitive nature can also leave lasting adverse effects on your health, wealth, and prosperity. As you design your future, EMBRACE not only where you are, but the fact that many others are likely on similar paths. Instead of seeing them as a threat, you can EMBRACE them as the spurs to greater self-development. Just keep in mind, we serve best through unity, not competition!

When you begin to recognize we are all on our paths, only then will you understand that your healthiest competitor is yourself. By competing with yourself and learning from others, you develop better listening skills, become more inclusive, and gain insights and inspiration from your experiences. You ultimately take unnecessary pressure off yourself and continue learning, creating, and growing. Do the best you can, even if it's in little chunks. As you let go of your comparisons and judgments, you'll begin to EMBRACE the real you. You will release tension and anxiety associated with rushing to the finish line, managing expectations, and following everyone else's lead. In addition, through your unique interior design, you can apportion avenues to NURTURE yourself and everything you value. When you include self-care and care of others, your design and life will flourish instead of leaving a ruthless path of ruin in blind pursuit of your wants and desires.

#31 the giant – through our desire to achieve, we may miss out on the sweetness and benefits of the smaller, more meaningful things in life.

NURTURE

*L*et's face it. You only have one vessel, your body, that contains the essential ingredients required for you to embark upon your ADVENTURES on Earth. NURTURE it and you will be prepared to leave an impacting and enriching legacy. You are also surrounded by people and things that bring value into your life. These too require care and feeding lest they disappear if you neglect them. Over time, our lack of self-care can generate disease and dysfunction and impact our ability to fully ENJOY our surroundings. While our observations and little voices can offer us clues, we often choose to disregard them. We chalk them up to genetics, diagnoses, and judgments and explain our way right out of tending to them. But there is hope at the end of the tunnel! Rather than make excuses for these shortfalls, we can focus on what is important, identify what may be needed, and start little routines to provide ourselves and others well-deserved attention and nourishment.

Most of us know why we struggle to care for ourselves and the valuable people and things in our lives. As you achieve small and large gains in caregiving, you increase the production of pleasure hormones, such as dopamine and serotonin. Through regulated activities, you will ENJOY your life more fully and better manage the challenging events that come with it. Ultimately, your health and wellbeing will always precede peace.

Be Healthy

Without your physical body, you would be hard-pressed to do literally anything. Your body needs nourishment, activity, rest, and relaxation. We get so caught up in doing that we often overlook our physical, mental, and emotional wellbeing. The fact is, your body is the most vital part of living. Don't tend to it, and you reduce your potential for success and ultimately your lifespan. NURTURE it and you enhance every aspect of your life!

Many of us take better care of our vehicles than we do of ourselves. What would you suppose would happen if you put substandard fuel and fluids in your car? Imagine also how it would perform without preventative care. Now, imagine leaving it constantly running, not tending to the electrical system, and never stopping the engine. WOW! That is what we do to ourselves when we ignore our health and wellbeing. Similar to autos, you will start to fall apart. Warning lights will come on, and you will begin to decline, deteriorate, and decay. By the time you realize what's happening, it is extremely difficult to fix. You will feel stranded. At least with a car, you have the option to purchase a new one. You cannot ditch your body and replace it. It is the only one you have. The best thing you can do is pay attention to the messages it offers, decide how you want it to perform, and create a routine to make it happen. Start taking care of yourself FIRST!

Consumption Assumption

We are what we digest! What you consume affects your body structure, bodily functions, and energy levels. To have the wherewithal to do as you please, you must give your body the care, feeding, and attention it needs. Nobody really needs to tell you what, when, or how to eat and drink as we all know the basics of nutrition. There's no doubt whether everything we consume contains a variety of fats, proteins, carbohydrates, and many other ingredients. What we need to keep in mind here is that everything you ingest moves through your body and creates your vessel. For most of us, this concept is not a new one. Your doctor or dietician can help you design a lifestyle eating plan that works for you.

Although the markets advertise a wide variety of diets, we already know how we feel when we finish eating and drinking certain things. You know about basic food and beverage nutrients, optimal portion sizes, and when to eat. Still, information bombards us, and ideas overwhelm and confuse us. By simply sticking to the basics provided below and deciding what will work best for your desired lifestyle, you will experience positive progressive results in your overall health and wellness!

First, consider food and liquid necessary to sustain life. Essential internal parts that require nourishment include structural tissues (connective tissues, bones) and organs (heart, lungs, stomach, intestines…even skin) that reinforce and sustain your outer body. You also have muscles and fat (energy reserves, warmth) to generate motion and protect these parts.

Finally, your biological fluids (blood, saliva, mucus, urine, etc.) lubricate and carry everything to various areas of your body. All of your internal body parts require suitable nourishment to function correctly and replenish. Take care of them, and they will take care of you through easier functioning and pain management.

Along with your physical body, your desired metabolism level must be fed. Consider how much you move around, stress levels, extreme weather conditions, illnesses/body repair, lifestyle, and environmental elements, such as smog, smoke, pollutants, parasites, etc. They all play a role in how much you must ingest to meet your energetic demands. For example, if you do not get enough sunshine, add more vitamin D. Low levels of vitamin D is one reason many folks fall ill in the winter when daylight is shorter. Another example is when you run out of energy, get testy, or are forgetful. Nutritionally, these circumstances often result from inadequate amounts of food, water, vitamins, and minerals.

When you pay attention to the clues your body reveals, you can NURTURE it with the ideal food, drink, or supplementation that works for you. As you begin making adjustments, consider too the type, amount, and frequency of when you feed yourself carbohydrates, fats, complete proteins, vitamins, and minerals. Since we all differ in size, metabolism, and activity levels, this can become very confusing and frustrating. As you make your body a priority, carefully experiment to discover what works well for you according to what you want to experience in your life. It is essential if you want your body to function well. Remember, you do not have to go it alone either. Nutritionists and other professionals can help.

No matter what route you take for your diet, consider these two rules of thumb. First pure, clear, and clean water is necessary to lubricate, transport, dissolve, and flush nutrients in your body. Not enough, and your cells cannot function properly. Excessive amounts can cause fatigue, brain damage, and other possible fatal effects by overloading your kidneys, offsetting electrolyte levels, and stressing your body. Balance is key! Next is sugar. It is in so much of what we consume and addictive! Too much of it, and you experience weight gain and interfere with blood pressure, liver, and brain functions. If you suffer from slow mental functions, an ability to remember and focus, or inflammation, reduce your sugar!

It is up to you to determine whether your diet aligns with what you want. If it currently is not, you have the power of choice to change it. If it is a mindset thing about the word diet, just remember, you are always on a diet. It is simply a word for what you put into your body. If you're confused about what to do, try different things through your sense of curiosity and ADVENTURE. Consider what worked in the past and modify it or find something completely new. Eventually, you will discover what works, and your body will naturally respond. As a result, you will feel more empowered and gain more control of your life.

Activity versus Exercise

It is crazy how merely mentioning diet and exercise can turn some people away. These terms can sound too constricting and too much like work. But really, not only do we all diet but we all exercise during our daily activities. To exercise is to actively move and make our bodies function. Indeed, some of us do it more often or intensely than others, but all who can move do so in some manner or another.

We all need a degree of activity to keep our muscles and bones strong, reduce health risks, and prolong our lives. Like everything, bodies in motion stay in motion until something, including thoughts and feelings, makes them stop. When you stop moving, many of your body parts in those areas receive less oxygen, blood, electrolytes, etc. Your inactivity may cause diabetes, cardiovascular disease, blood clots, osteoporosis, chronic pain, and many other diseases in your body. It can also lessen your immune system and mess with your thyroid and metabolism. These ailments are why it is so important to keep your body in motion. Move to live a longer, healthier life, even if it starts with baby steps of a new VENTURE!

We all have different life ambitions. Some people love to do activities that require physical exertion. Others simply want a healthy lifestyle, optimal weight, and ideal energy levels. No matter what your goal is, you must be clear with it to get moving and make it happen. Take a different approach to exercise, activity, and movement. Change your thoughts and feelings about exercise, and you will change your life. For example, you'll act

> *Play your own motivational mind games and make up your own rules that encourage you to take action and create wins, big and small.*

lazy if you think and say you're lazy. What would happen if you thought you were energetic, enthusiastic, or even organized? If you think you're too busy, you'll act like you're too busy. What would happen if you felt like you were in control of your calendar, time, or schedule? You are your thoughts; it's as simple as that!

Another way to alter your thoughts and feelings about exercise and movement is to align your activities to your values. As you AWAKEN, your values will become more apparent. Keep in mind, you'll either want to honor them through pleasure or protect them from pain. If your activity does not support the pleasure or pain of a deep value, you reduce your level of motivation, effort, and commitment. For example, if you value freedom and struggle to move around freely, you can move away from that pain by including walks and other slow motions into your daily routines until you start to move with ease. The results you experience will likely entice you to move toward doing more. Take the same approach and you will continue to advance your physical health. It is never too late. Start slow and keep moving. Experimentation and repetition are the keys!

Sometimes we experience competing values where other activities seem more important. This conflict masks the necessity of doing activities that improve our health and wellbeing. We allow our excuses to get in the way, and we end up working harder for others than we do for ourselves. Like all goals, even your best intentions can go awry when you do not make them a priority. Do not allow everything and everyone else's priorities to take precedence over your health. If it is recognition, appreciation, and other external stimulating responses you desire, you'll get that when people notice how well you are taking care of yourself and how much happier you are. There is nothing wrong with wanting positive feedback as it can motivate you to take action and better care of yourself. Consider this. If you do not take care of yourself, you will not have the capacity to care for others anyway. Life hands us enough stressful moments. Let's not add to them by intensifying them with health problems.

> *Make yourself a priority in all areas of your health and wellness! You owe it to yourself to maintain your health. In addition to making life easier for you, you'll foster the best in others.*

Rest Assured

Naps are so underrated! The fact is, most of us don't get adequate sleep at night. It is so bad that we now have sleep monitors with wearable fitness gear to measure our rest. We all know sleep and rest have many health benefits, yet we ignore their importance. Think about those days when you didn't get enough sleep. The next day, you were probably moody, forgetful, unproductive, and stressed. Keep it up, and over time we put on unwanted weight, reduce our sex drive, and become more prone to illnesses. Over long periods, we might contract diabetes, heart disease, high blood pressure, or stroke. Our bodies must rest so they can heal, replenish, and store memories - all for strength, stamina, and growth to carry out our purpose.

As your body rests, it repairs itself. Although it takes 7-10 years to replace nearly all of your cells, your body parts constantly shed and renew cells at different intervals. The best time for this to happen is nighttime while you rest. As you sleep, your miraculous body takes over and heals itself. Not only does your body heal, but so does your mind. Sleep and rest allow you to tap into your imagination, channel your memories for learning, gain clarity in thought, and improve responsiveness. Through this, you reduce your stress and increase your creativity. As you can see, your physical and mental vitality relies on sufficient rest. But how much…

Sometimes it's hard to determine the amount of sleep and rest that is right for us, yet it's essential if we want to feel refreshed and energized. Several sleep studies are out there with various conclusions about how much sleep and rest we should be getting daily. People sleep an average of 7-9 hours while others sleep intermittently and get 3 hours of sleep 3 times per day. Some people need much more sleep than the recommended 9 hours. Once again, our bodies all operate differently. As you test what works best for you, you will know how much rest you need and how many hours of sleep you should get to function at your best.

> Rest your mind and body. Sleep can rejuvenate your entire being and aid in your most optimal performance.

Here are a couple of pointers to consider in the meantime. If your physical, emotional, or mental demands are high, schedule a time to go to bed earlier and stick to it as best as possible. Like growing kids, your body needs to repair, and your mind needs to clear for the next day. When that does not fit into your calendar, test your ability to nap and see how it can work into a healthy sleep cycle for you. Carve out some time, grab eye covering and earplugs and stretch out in a comfortable place. Some people benefit from a 15-minute power nap to a one-hour snooze. These short naps can refresh your mind, increase your energy level, and enhance your attitude. My garage was a perfect place to snooze after a ride home from work. I would turn off the car, close the garage door, kick the seat back, and let the sleep take over. When I opened my eyes, I knew I was done. I also used to go out to my car during lunch break on cold days, lean the seat back, and enjoy the sun shining in the windshield as I snoozed. I found that I was much more productive and relaxed when I went back into work. Never underestimate the power of a good nap!

Ironically, it can take some effort to get some rest. All of our health habits can impact our sleep. Even putting off sleep can lead to higher stress hormones that make sleep more difficult. It can be a vicious cycle. Pay attention so you can figure out what works best for you. In the meantime, do your best to not neglect other healthy habits that can prolong your life. They deserve some of your attention, too!

Law of Rhythm – Everything has a natural cycle or rhythm in the universe.

Buckle Down

Our bodies are such amazing specimens. They let us know what is going on inside and out but only if we pay attention to them. Impacts on things like dental, hearing, and eyesight can play a major factor in our health. Our internal and external organs, including our most expansive organ, skin, have vital jobs. By cleaning, protecting, and nourishing them, they will continue to function properly and bolster their health to alleviate as many ailments as possible.

Lower the volume on your technology. It encourages you to listen more closely and saves you from damaging your ears.

Regular self-care, along with physician visits, can offer you an awareness of what your body is telling you it needs. Other healthy habits, such as using sunscreen, sex protection, seat belts, helmets, and other protective items, can help sustain your health. Although some of these are laws,

#43 dental hygiene – demonstrate self-care by conquering dis-ease before it starts, including what's in your mouth and what comes out of it.

following them is still a personal choice. Remember, you can prepare for risks by investigating the pros and cons of each and deciding from there, or you can jump right in. Regardless of your decision, be mindful not to fall victim to your own rebellion without considering the consequences.

You have a responsibility to care for the vessel designed to care for you. When you sacrifice your health, you not only put yourself in jeopardy, but you reduce your ability to actively function and fully participate in life. Remember what flight attendants say in their airplane safety brief. When you put your mask on first, you will be better prepared to respond and more capable of serving others. The same can be said for your own health and wellness.

Be Well

If you are sick and tired of being sick and tired, you may want to consider NURTURING your unseen aspects of wellness, called energy. The lessons you gained from past stressful situations can help you create the wellness you deserve. Stress is such a huge portion of our lives as even the smallest things can cause us stress. The problem is not about having stressful thoughts and feelings. It is whether you deal with them promptly. Some stress, called eustress, is good for you. Like what happens when you achieve a goal, the excitement it brings raises your heart rate, pleasure hormones, and motivation. You have a tendency to grow and feel satisfied afterward. On the other hand, long-term distress can wreak havoc on your nervous system and create mental, emotional, and physical diseases, disorders, and dysfunctions. When we hold onto stress, we struggle to find a way to release the energy tied to it. You may feel uneasy, overwhelmed, and sometimes even worthless. It's as if you're losing control. All of us have experienced this to some degree at one time or another. When you learn to manage your thoughts and feelings during taxing situations, you naturally reduce your stress levels and become more creative. With higher creativity, you will find it easier to solve the problems that caused the stress in the first place.

Thoughts Become Things

Human beings are such critical thinkers. We do our best to make sense of and understand information to figure out our world and our place in it. Our inquisitiveness can also generate questions about our past and moving forward. It's what we do to create the lives we want. Our thinking is tied to our emotions and can become problematic when we internalize stories that spark doubt, fear, sadness, guilt, and other negative feelings. We naturally slip into survival mode when we sense harm, even if we will not be hurt. If we do not confront these negative thoughts, ailments will ensue.

The pressure we put on ourselves to achieve goals, follow schedules, and meet deadlines is real for us. When we do not follow our plans or live up to others' expectations, we end up violating values of integrity, reliability, and consistency. The ridicule we face from this violation and ourselves plays in our heads and can be damaging. It does not matter if you are a superstar or a failure. All of us are subject to criticism of right, wrong, and good, bad. It's about how you react to it and what you learn in the process. The fact is, we are all human and make mistakes. Once you EMBRACE that, you will be able to relax a little and know your failures are merely feedback that contains lessons for growth.

It's time we stop the insane negative message loops that create distortions, imbalances, and disturbances. Otherwise, you will think yourself right into disease, disorders, and dysfunctions. James Allen, in his book, *As a Man Thinketh*, states that "Disease and health, like circumstances, are rooted in thought. Sickly thoughts will express themselves through a sickly body." Be honest with your thoughts and use them wisely. Your ill bodily symptoms are merely clues for you to recognize that what you are thinking, feeling, and doing are unhelpful. Now is the best time to choose a better approach to your stress before your stress sends you on an unwanted path. Do not delay. Peace is knocking at your front door!

Sheer Energy

We are pure energy. Energy is what holds our body masses together, makes our bodies function, and helps us perform tasks. As you can imagine, it is one of the most essential pieces that you must NURTURE for yourself – and others. It is so important because not only does it exist all throughout our bodies, but it also extends outward from our bodies. You see, energy has no boundaries and permeates everything. It moves quickly through the air in waves that touch every one of us.

We are not simply energy consumers. Our bodies are also energy-producing machines! According to holistic healers, we have five layers of energy: physical, etheric, emotional, mental, and spiritual. Simply stated, your energy is your aura and is affected by thoughts, feelings, consumption, activity levels, and environmental factors. Too much unused energy stored in our bodies, regardless of its form, can become toxic. For example, body fat is an energy store and, as such, must be used. If too much of it is stored in our bodies, we can contract diseases, such as diabetes, stroke, heart disease, and cancer, among others. When your thoughts generate too much stress for too long, your immunities lower and leave you vulnerable to producing illness, i.e., heart disease, depression, stomach problems, asthma, and so on.

On the outside of your body, animals can feel your energy right away and instinctively sense your fear, sadness, joy, confidence, anger, and so on. People in your surroundings can feel your energy when you are excited, sad, angry, etc. People can also project their energy onto you. Our exposure to toxic energetic environments can be challenging. When you are not aware that they are having an effect on you or you do not get away from them, that negative energy can adversely impact you and your life. That is why it's good to surround yourself with people who have higher levels of energy. They will help bring yours up to healthier levels. I am not merely talking about energetic activities, but their aura.

As we Scientists, medical doctors, psychologists, and the like discovered that our energy input and output contribute to various diseases. Cancer, ulcers, gout, migraines, heart attacks, diabetes, backaches, strokes, among many others, are all influenced by our energy consumption and production. Once again, this is where our body deviates from ease and creates disease. You are individually responsible for managing your energy, including everything from what you put into your body, to your activity level, to what you think and feel about others. Your energy cues show up in your actions, appearance, and resulting actions of others. As you pay attention to these factors, you can determine how to best NURTURE your energy and yourself. Self-care is vital to maintaining a high energetic aura and optimal wellness. Since energy affects everything in your life, you will be glad you took time for self-care!

> **Law of Compensation - You are responsible for the energy you release into the universe. Rest assured that it will always boomerang back to you.**

Putting Energy to Work

Emotions play an integral role in our physical, mental, and energetic areas of wellness. Remember, emotion is your energy in action. We all develop unique ways of releasing it based on thoughts and feelings in our past. For example, people may cry at weddings, funerals, celebrations, or other events based on their sense of love, loss, or excitement that generates energy around love, sadness, joy, etc. The experience induced a memory that created a feeling and generated energy. Crying is how the energy was released - or emoted. Another example is when people laugh out of humor, discomfort, relief, or anger. Each feeling has its individual energy. You put that energy into motion through your unique expressions.

Some of us are more in touch with our feelings than others. Our emotions are evident when being expressed both individually and in conjunction with others. Although we often assume the reason behind these emotions, we rarely understand them. When you make the effort to comprehend and use them wisely, emotions can be excellent tools. Emotions can also cause trouble in various ways, especially when we allow them to bottle up inside. Long-held negative emotions generate stress, distractions, disturbances, and disruptions that turn into disappointments, discouragement, and disagreements. Those contribute to disease, disorder, and dysfunction in your body and outer world. Long suppressed emotions are trapped

> *Use emotions as catalysts for success. Short-term, low-level energy motivates us to get things done and can be useful as long as it is not burdensome on others. Harness it, let go of it, and EMBRACE new feelings tied to achievement.*

within the confines of our bodies and if not released, will affect our wellness and very likely the welfare of others. Let's say a couple has a spat that does not get resolved. It will fester and build inside one or both until someone snaps or until it causes an uneasiness resulting in ill health.

Habitual emotions, expressed or not, affect the formation of our cells and create positive and negative vibrations. The emotion that receives the most attention becomes the dominant energy and usually overcomes the weaker energy. Therefore, if you think and feel negatively consistently, that negative energy will outweigh your positive energy. The same can be said for positive energy. In turn, it will build up in your body and affect everything else in your surroundings.

If you prefer more positive experiences, this is where the power of positive thinking and feeling comes into play. It's unrealistic and unfair to ourselves to think we can "just get over it." If you're struggling with negativity, do something physically productive – and tie it to a value. By creating positive actions, you naturally produce endorphins which drive positive emotions. After a while of generating these emotions, they become stronger and overpower the weaker ones. This switch allows negativity to flow through you while you take on a more positive attitude. You can probably imagine that this cycle generates more optimism and continues as you form a new productive habit. Get your body moving!

Some people frown on others who practice expressing positive emotions. Acting positively does not mean that your other emotions are invalid and should be denied. We will all feel sad, happy, angry, joyful, guilty, etc. The point is, if you are affected by something, you must use constructive channels to allow it flow through your body. You can also neutralize it through balanced emotions and reason so you can move past it. Do not allow negative energies to linger and impact your wellness. Remember, whatever it is will pass, but only if we allow it. Take a breath and have faith in yourself!

Law of Duality - Everything has its opposite. All structures must have two sides to exist. With negative situations, you can eventually create positive outcomes. Without tension, you will not have many opportunities to reach your full potential for growth. But do not hold on to negativity. Rather, let it flow through you.

Just Breathe

Your breath is your lifeline! It is as essential as your heartbeat. Interestingly enough, we often do not even think about it because it's automatic. Usually, we only notice it when we feel short of breath. Yet, it is an accurate indicator of our health and wellbeing levels. It seems logical that as an essential part of living, we would pay attention to it. But, like everything else that is automatic, many of us take it for granted.

We all know that breathing oxygen is good for your health. Your breath is also an indicator telling you how well you NURTURE your body, mind, emotions, and energy. Naturally, our increased breath will let us know when we exert energy. The more we exert ourselves, the harder and faster we breathe. No brainer, right? Some people are conscious of their breathing and can control it during invigorating activities. By learning to consciously manage your breath, you can improve your physical form, clear your mental focus, and experience feelings of confidence. If you ignore your breath during intense

> *Breathe from your belly. Belly breathing helps you control your emotions. Kids instinctively do it when they're excited, engaged, and focused. Upset children breathe from the top of their chest and struggle to function and talk. Calmed down, they breathe from their bellies and can talk again. Take note from the children out there, and don't forget to breathe!*

activities, you may experience unwanted symptoms such as reduced physical abilities, scattered thoughts, emotional apathy, exhaustion, and confusion. Recognize the symptoms and consider if your exertion needs adjusting or proper breathing can be the cure.

While fitness levels and breath can dictate how well we perform, unhealthy stress levels can also negatively impact breathing and performance. As we experience stress, our breathing difficulty intensifies and becomes harder to control. This sign tells you to be aware of what is going on with your body, mind, and energy. Additionally, when we are doing something and doubt ourselves, we tend to breathe more erratically and shallower. You may be pushing harder than usual, have fabricated thoughts and feelings of inadequacy, or require more food, drink, or rest. That is

> *Inhale clean air deeply and fully to help relieve anxiety and create a relaxed feeling.*

your sign to do something different. You will know whether you should push through or pause to replenish your energy intake so you do not risk injuring yourself. Intentional breathing empowers you to make the best choice in each situation.

Be Kind

We are such social creatures. We ENJOY surrounding ourselves with family, friends, and colleagues who bring out the best in us. Quite frankly, we all need human contact and interaction. As we NURTURE our health and wellbeing, we certainly will want to do the same with our valuable relationships. The challenge is that, since we all are different, our opinions can sometimes get in the way of the value our relationships bring. Sadly, if this happens often enough, we end up alone and lonely.

Our relationship matrices are very complex filled with family, close friends, associates, and many others. All of them hold varying degrees of closeness. As such, each requires its individual level of attention and respect. Lopsided relationships are very challenging and can be physically, mentally, and emotionally exhausting. It is up to each of us to know which ones are valuable and seek to understand their needs. As you consider your important relationships, pay attention to the feedback they offer so you can continue to develop yourself. You will find it quite difficult to offer others what you have not found in yourself!

A Family Affair

Our family members are often the most influential people in our lives. They taught us, left lasting impressions, and helped us develop our personalities and ideas about society. Our childhood development was also influenced by close ties with friends from social groups, schools, and communities. In adulthood, we used what we learned to create new families, form lasting bonds through personal relationships and work, and watched others fade away.

Family-type relationships are deep and very distinct from casual ones. Because we approach our relationships with individual wants, problems, and energy, the deeper relationships tend to bring us the most pleasure along with the most pain. We naturally know which ones are the closest and we value the most. We think about them, feel the urge to stay connected, and, more often than not, have a desire to treat them with love, compassion, and respect. Although we project our own needs onto our family members, we often overlook theirs. Over time, this disconnect can severely damage our relationships. People also have a hard time grasping others' needs even when they are expressed. As a result, the struggle continues. After endless arguments, neglect, and finger-pointing, we end up wondering what happened as the relationship dies. The odd thing is, more often than not, we know what happened. At some point, we may finally recognize the role we played, but we can't let it stop there. We must take responsibility for our part. Do not wait until it's too late to NURTURE your valuable family-type relationships. If you do, you may find they have moved on without you or pushed you away.

Know which relationships are meaningful and provide them the best care. Just like plants, if you do not NURTURE them, they wither away. By giving a plant all that it needs, it will flourish and produce in abundance. Your valuable relationships are the same. They require commitment, mutual support, acceptance, and above all, love. A plant will not thrive unless you know how much sunlight, water, nutrients, and attention it requires. For those requiring a lot of attention and NURTURING, decide how you can best include their care-giving in your life and share the level of effort with others.

Walter Darring

#20 big sister – all of our family members influenced us in one way or another. Fortunately, and sometimes unfortunately, the close you are, the more they impact you.

All relationships bring varying degrees of value and joy, so know what that is ahead of time. Not every bond is mutually beneficial and supportive. When you learn what the relationship needs, you can evaluate whether it is worth your time and energy and how much you want it to grow. Some family members may only want small amounts of contact and limited interaction. Let go of your desire for close attachment and commit to a level that they can handle. Give a plant too much water, and you may drown it. Here is where you assess the amount of effort you want to provide and gently work with them from there. Once again, be clear in what you mutually want out of your close, intimate, and deep relationships or they may otherwise become acquaintances.

I experienced this firsthand throughout my military career. I was so focused on my life that I rarely connected with my family. We didn't have the communications devices or social media we do today. Long-distance phone calls were expensive and not convenient in places like Cuba. On one of the few occasions I visited with family, I broke down in tears. My sister, Kris, chuckled awkwardly and asked why I was crying. I could not explain the guilt inside, so I just laughed and said I didn't know. The fact is, I had not seen Kris for years, nor had I seen her daughters since they were babies. All I could think of was our times together as little girls and how much I missed her. We loved to play together and make funny faces at each other. Those days were long gone, and here we were, standing together as adults. We celebrated our visit and ENJOYED some long-lost family bonding. Over time, we've mutually EMBRACED our infrequent contacts and cherish the blips in time when we do connect. We love each other just the way we are, and both of us know that whenever we connect, our relationship will continue to flourish.

Hang Loose

We interact with so many people on a regular basis, many of which are not of our choosing. Basically, these acquaintances, such as peer groups, colleagues, or community members, engage with us by virtue of our surroundings and shared interests. We intentionally interact with them but for shorter periods and specific purposes. Most of the time, they require much less effort, and we suffer no significant loss when they break away. Yet, similar to all relationships, you still need to NURTURE them to perform specific roles, complete work effectively, and ENJOY your experience while in their presence. The network you create can add substantial value to your life when done effectively. People step up and help each other all of the time. Be courteous, friendly, and gracious before you need them. Otherwise, you will end up standing alone.

Professionals we hire, such as, physicians, building contractors, lawyers, financial advisors, and such, are also loose, infrequent connections. Because you chose them to perform a service for you, they require a certain degree of openness and transparency from you. You will certainly want to develop and NURTURE these relationships as they enter your private world on a limited basis. Each needs respectful, candid, and clear communications so they can offer you their best service. Do not expect to receive high-quality care and service if you neglect to NURTURE your relationship with those you hire.

Moreover, make sure the communications go both ways by listening to their expert advice and asking questions, so you both understand what needs to be accomplished. Otherwise, you might not receive the results you expect and experience more difficulties than desired. This may seem like a no-brainer, but we see it happen all of the time. I have experienced plenty of miscommunication problems from not fostering my relationships. They left scars and stories to help me learn to better communicate. Here's one that actually worked well for me.

The first home I bought was a small rancher. I lived in it for many years and decided it was time for an upgrade. I wanted an open floor plan, so I hired a contract company to remodel the whole kitchen, living room, and dining room. When the businessman showed up, I told him what I wanted and discussed the various options. The businessman was a knowledgeable, very well-spoken professional with a talented crew of contractors. His team came in, tore down walls, ripped out windows, replaced old cabinets and fixtures, opened everything up, and made the remodeling magic happen. I was delighted until a couple of days later. I reached under the sink and felt water on the cabinet floor. I wasn't sure if it was a leaky pipe or something wrong with the sink, so I called the contract company. The businessman was very accommodating and sent his team to check it out. They didn't detect anything, yet I continued to find water under the sink. After the third returned visit, one of the contractors figured it out. When they used the sprayer, water would follow the hose all of the way down and drip under the sink. We were all relieved. Although the team was a bit frustrated with the situation, they graciously came out until they resolved the problem. Shared respect and patience were vital in the ENJOYABLE outcome.

Just Get Along

The relationships that probably challenge us the most are the ones we do not necessarily want but maintain for the sake of someone or something else. Examples include former spouses, other people's friends, past business partners, certain family members, and so on. We all have difficult or complex relationships in our lives that we choose to keep. Typically, it is because we share something valuable. The problem is one or both parties unconsciously hold onto thoughts and feelings of the past. Our emotions arise each time we interact with them and become barriers to our ability to cooperate for a common cause. The fact is, if we want the best outcome later, we need to figure out how to NURTURE it. If we do not, we will struggle to maintain a stable connection with what we value.

These types of scenarios happen most often between divorced parents. Coordinating time, finances, medical emergencies, and many other details were hard enough when together. As they separate, the arguments often continue and are projected onto the children. Add a stepparent and situations get really complex. Since children are sponges, they soak it all up and use it later as part of their life's strategy. When a NURTURED relationship fits its new purpose, the conversations and coordination become easier. The children may also benefit by learning how to hold constructive conversations. The ease in communications is one reason many couples with failed marriages become better friends than lovers. But if either one holds onto their past emotions, the struggles remain.

> ✎ *Resolve your issues, or you will dissolve your relationships. If your relationship is important, make NURTURING it a priority. If it does not bring you value, don't waste either of your time, be THANKFUL for it, and let it fade. This will allow you to make space for new, more meaningful relationships.*

We simply need to remember that we cannot control others. We can only control ourselves and experiment in ways to improve those relationships. Our role in each is different, as is the degree of attention. The value we seek in them determines the amount of effort required to NURTURE them. It's up to all people in the relationship to determine what that can be. We do not have to get along to go along or go along to get along. We have the power and freedom of choice to decide who and what we want in our lives. Want something different, do something different. Regardless, it all takes some level of care and effort.

Be Gentle

People are only one aspect of our surroundings that we NURTURE. We love being amongst our stuff. It is how we identify ourselves individually. Everything we own satisfies some certain value, or at least it did in the past. Otherwise, why would we keep it? Think about it. Your household and everything attached to it is what you have earned and often are proud to claim. When the newness wanes and your focus shifts to the next great ADVENTURE, the old stuff naturally takes a back seat. The reality is, when we get so busy, we tend to let things slip, pile up, and get out of hand. After a while, the value our belongings once held becomes a burden. Neglect them, and, just like relationships, they typically fade away, maybe sooner than we would hope. Consciously choose to NURTURE them, and they will continue to provide lasting value. Ultimately, the fate of your belongings is up to you.

Home Sweet Home

There is such a joy in settling into a home of our own. It provides you and your family with a sense of safety and security. When you first move in, it's open and ready for your belongings. You have the freedom to choose how you want to live in it and how your household will operate. At that moment, you have the comfort of knowing you are right where you belong. Your home has so many ways of trying to get your attention, and they are often overlooked or put off until they become an emergency. We all know a neglected home can be very costly and cause stress. It signals you through fading colors, stains, splintering wood, or peeling paint. These signs also extend to the quirkiness you experience in appliances, fixtures, and pipes. Without regular maintenance, you will find yourself uncomfortable and stressed in your own home. Your once-lovely home now feels like a hassle and money pit. It's tough to ENJOY the serenity your home is supposed to bring when chaos threatens your feelings of safety and security. Regular upkeep is very important. You and your family's life are worth it. There is nothing like being in the comfort of your own home, but it takes a proactive approach to make it feel that way.

As an extension of your home, all of your belongings need some degree of attention, including whatever helps you get around, tools, clothing, toys, etc. We can get so focused on daily routines that we forget about our belongings. If neglected, they too will fall apart, become obsolete, and no longer add value. That's certainly a problem if you need them for your livelihood in the various areas of your life, like home and work. When neglected, we undoubtedly disrupt our world. By the same token, if they are worth keeping, they should be worth the maintenance, upgrades, and daily upkeep. Otherwise, it might be a good idea to pass them on and make room in our lives for our own new ADVENTURES.

Although this may seem basic, we all have things in our life that we neglect. The key here is to be aware and assess what to do with them. When you NURTURE your home and valuables in them, you will have peace of mind and a sense of organization. You will be prepared and make space for a life you love. You will also be better prepared to respond to any surprise mishaps that happen from time to time. As a result, your residences will offer a lasting sense of safety and security. Your tools, equipment, and toys will operate efficiently and last up to and possibly through their lifecycle. When your surroundings are in order, you save time while reducing heartache and frustration. You can relax and ENJOY the comfort of your own home a little more.

These concepts can also be helpful in your professional world. Here's how they can apply to businesses as well. Once you start your business and it grows, check and service your assets regularly. Your machinery, tools, and technology must be maintained to ensure they are useable, reliable, and sustainable for long term operations. Review financial resources to confirm you are on track with your business income and budget. Groom your workforce regularly with things like leadership opportunities, continuing education and training, and recognition to promote retention. NURTURE everything in your business on a routine basis and keep a finger on its pulse to assess its health. Finally, if it is not working out as expected, be courageous enough to release your grip on it and choose what will work better. EMBRACING this approach will reduce stress and help you focus on the core of your business.

Money Matters

Money can be such a powerful tool. Although nobody really knows who created it, it maintains a dominant energetic force in the world. It can add joy and abundance into our lives and can also generate fear, anxiety, regret, etc. Therefore, we would be wise to pay attention to and NURTURE it so we can reap the greatest rewards.

Money is similar to any other energetic force in that it must flow efficiently. Remember from your science class that anything at rest stays at rest until some force puts it into motion. Also, anything in motion stays in motion until a force changes it. Your individual success with money is all about keeping it in flow while balancing the amount you want to regularly circulate and how much you want to store for your future desires.

Law of Vibration - Keep energy in motion to stay alive and intentional, or it will leave you and transform elsewhere. While in motion, we will attract similar vibrational frequencies. Take Note!

Our greatest problem with money is that it can be a heavy burden for some people, and the energy we individually apply toward it can be scary and overwhelming. Our thoughts and feelings about money will guide us in how we handle it. Similar to anything unfamiliar to us, if we do not have an opportunity to experience its goodness, some of us may believe it is evil. As we become more comfortable with handling money, we will better understand its positive power. With this in mind, we will be best served when we respect its influence and are aware of how we respond to it. The synergistic power it creates can extend to anyone who flows with it, holds positive energy toward it, and NURTURES it.

See money as a means, not the only way. It is simply a small aspect of measured success, so consider every part of your life when determining your success factor.

Every one of us develops our own strategies to spend, save, and invest money based on what we know and what is important to us. Our aim should always be to give its energy toward what we value and what brings joy for the long haul. If you aimlessly spend your money, you may end up with stuff you do not want or very little left to put toward what you do want in the future. NURTURE your energy around money, and the results will NURTURE you.

Best Buds

We cannot talk about NURTURE and not include our pets. Our animals are often the most wonderful beings in our lives. From dogs and cats to lizards and fish, we can form a deep bond with them. For the most part, they love unconditionally, want so much to please us, and become integral parts of the family. They can even keep a secret! Although their instinct is for love and survival, many of them still ENJOY training and serving a purpose. No matter the reason, when we invite living beings into our homes, we are responsible for NURTURING them.

For some people, this is easy and a given. For others, they may not have initially considered the time, energy, and space necessary to care for them properly. Therefore, as we touched on in VENTURE, if you have animals or want to add them to your family, choose the ones that fit your lifestyle before including them into your family so you can give them proper care. Consider your home, activity level, purpose, family members, travel, etc. These factors help you narrow down the type, size, age, temperament, and maintenance associated with potential pets before choosing.

Along with companionship, our pets require much of the same functional care we humans do. Social interaction, nutrition, exercise, and cleanliness are the basic needs. They will also need a degree of training, dental checkups, and basic healthcare. Here is a quick point to remember. Everyone is responsible for the animal that lives in a home, not just the person who brought it home or received it. This point can be beneficial when deciding which pets to consider for your children.

Kids can manage animals that require little skill or effort, like hamsters or fish. These pets offer children the chance to develop and demonstrate basic caregiving skills they already know. Give them exotic pets, like certain snakes, birds, lizards, or even dogs and cats and you will find the care, training, and feeding will boomerang back to the adult. The experience will likely be beyond their abilities, and both the pet and child will struggle to ENJOY the ADVENTURE. Make sure everyone knows and is capable of performing their roles. Sharing the duties allows all parties to ENJOY a life of companionship together.

It is not that we do not know the importance of caring for ourselves and others. It's that we often do not practice it to the degree we would prefer. You only have so much energy to expend each day. If you do not channel that energy toward what is important to you, you will feel overwhelmed when trying to care for everyone and everything. You will either wear yourself out or not do anything at all. By NURTURING yourself, you create healthy energy that you can devote to what you value and carry out your ikigai. Align your energy and values with all of your relationships, invest appropriate levels of care for them, and let the destructive relationships fade. Be gentle and kind no matter who or what the circumstances. Life is too short to live in discomfort. It only takes one small, consistent step at a time to positively impact your health, wellness, and surroundings. You will be THANKFUL that you did!

THANK

G ratitude is one of the most valuable tools we can use to create happiness. By appreciating where we are and what we have now, we can let go of the stress of wanting something else. As we express THANKS over time, it can bring greater confidence, improved wellness, and long-lasting relationships. We have so much to be grateful for. Think about how abundant life is. Even if you do not have everything you want right now, you can be THANKFUL for what you do have, EMBRACE the joy of your life, and open yourself up to a more ENJOYABLE future.

By showing appreciation for all of your experiences, you will begin to see the richness and use them to create an even brighter future. Everything you learn, create, and teach has beautiful gifts waiting for you to discover. Once you learn how to find and begin to use them, you will release unwanted ties to your past, open yourself up to new possibilities, and have the power to EMBRACE life's ADVENTURES toward mastery in the future.

Law of Gratitude - The more you give, the more you receive.

Gratitude in Lessons

Sometimes we have a tendency to overlook the lessons of our past and take them for granted. We may wish we had done something completely different than the route we had taken. But to understand the reason events occurred can offer you invaluable lessons to help you shape your ability to create something different now and for the future. The events of your past do not make you a horrible human or less than anyone else. They offer you opportunities to learn the passion and desire you have been using to express your earthly purpose with meaning. Stop beating yourself and others up about the past so we all can EMBRACE our uniqueness and use our lessons for the greater good.

Humanness

All things happen for a reason. Each experience is our opportunity to learn something. We do our best when we use the lessons and experiment with life. When things go well, or we squeak by, we usually give THANKS with ease. While some folks tell us to leave our past behind, its rich lessons enhance our lives today. We get so caught up in the anguish of past mistakes, ours and others, that it is challenging to be grateful. The funny thing is, we are supposed to experience human errors and challenges.

Let's face it, all of us have had moments of indiscretion or impulsiveness that led to unwanted consequences. If you have yet to learn from your past, when you recall the events, you will feel the intensity of the emotions until you extract the lessons. The more intense your feelings, the more you have to learn from it. The same goes for pleasant as well as disappointing experiences. How do they differ? Pleasant ones will be incentives for you to do it over. Whether you're aware of them or not, you continue to behave like this as long as you get what you want. Disappointing experiences initially push you into your survival behaviors of fight, flight, freeze, or conform. If you do not create a strategy to resolve it, you will cling to guilt, shame, anger, fear, sadness, or other unhelpful emotions until you do.

Be THANKFUL that you have such a robust system to work for you. It can keep us out of danger, help us live harmoniously, and guide us toward our purpose. Regardless of the incompatible relationships, conflicting career choices, and depleted bank accounts, we have a powerful brain to help us figure out our options. Through gratitude, you will be less stressed and better prepared to handle unexpected challenges with tried and true or new solutions. As a bonus, once you learn to be THANKFUL for your humanness, you will be able to graciously extend the same to others.

> ✒ *Start a gratitude journal. In it, offer THANKS for all of your past lessons, your current value-added creations, and your future desires. This is the secret to start creating a future you desire.*

Fellow Humans

The constant cycle of people coming in and out of our lives offers us so much to appreciate. They are with us from beginning to end and help us learn how to cooperate, coordinate, and collaborate. People help us learn the basic needs of feeling secure, safe, loved, and belonging. They also offer outlets to demonstrate our confidence, achievement, respect, and sense of uniqueness. Above all, people inspire our creativity, spontaneity, purpose, acceptance, meaning, and morality. The people in our lives are a direct reflection of ourselves and a result of how we view and treat the world. Without others, we would struggle to grow, express ourselves, and aspire to be our best. The sad thing is, we usually do not recognize their impact and, as such, do not adequately NURTURE our relationships with them or demonstrate THANKS.

People offer us so many reasons to be grateful, from gifts and deeds to the lessons that go along with them. When you give THANKS to the many people in your life, you will develop a positive, energetic bond with them and yourself. You will realize the gifts in their intentions and give up any expectations. Most people want to help others succeed and be their best. With that in mind, extend your gratitude toward every person that passes your way. They offer you opportunities to learn more about yourself, sharpen your focus, and create ADVENTURES you will never want to forget.

Forgotten Treasures

One of the best aspects of being human is we will always want for something. Wanting can be advantageous in that it offers you something to strive for. It motivates us and may provide us with treasures to enhance our lives or create new experiences. Even the most basic treasures of food, water, clothes, shelter, and other essentials are things we will make concerted efforts to get. When we have them, we are often tempted to take them for granted instead of being grateful.

Some people complain about what they had when they were growing up when in reality, offering THANKS would be more beneficial. Our homes, playgrounds, schools, and neighborhoods all aided in our development and growth. They shaped our independence, social skills, and tolerance for risk. They also continue to hold a treasure chest of golden nuggets in lessons that you can use today to get what you want, even if it's something totally different. Offering THANKS for what you once had can also free you from negative emotions of regret, humiliation, remorse, etc. and open your eyes to new creative possibilities. It's powerful!

The most pleasurable treasures are easiest to appreciate because you know the value of these. Yet, over time, we even take those for granted, that is until they are practically gone. If you want to test whether or not you cherish something, take a moment to picture life without it. Your feelings will signify whether to NURTURE or let go of it. You will discover a renewed energy for what you keep and graciousness toward what you let go. Either way, extend THANKS to your treasures because they served you along your path.

> *Law of Environmental Manifestation – Every single thing around you is an extension of you, derived from your attitude and beliefs system.*

What Had Happened

Regardless of their intensity, activities in our past also generate golden nuggets from which we can learn. Even our most minor actions can rock our worlds and provide big lessons through the joy or pain we experience. Actions like birth and death, celebratory moments and mistakes, and times of joy and those of devastation deserve our THANKS for the rich lessons they presented.

Events may come to you intentionally or by surprise, and they, along with people and objects in our surroundings, all play into how you created strategies to live today. Every good and destructive nugget in life can teach you about your habits, talents, risk tolerances, and other activities you've adopted and shared with others. As you EMBRACE an attitude of gratitude, you will begin to see both sides of what actions have to offer. THANKFULNESS is a powerful tool that can help bring about greater wisdom and smooth imbalanced emotions with less effort through reason.

Our lives are like a schoolhouse from which to learn. Any forward movements you experience are derived from lessons you learned in your past. You created it, the good, the bad, the stress, the calm, all of it. EMBRACE this idea. If you still struggle to give THANKS to the lessons from your past actions, maybe you're still holding onto the connected emotions. This burden can be draining.

One way to let go of these unsupportive emotions is by practicing the art of forgiveness toward yourself and others. Slow down for a moment. Start giving THANKS to every experience you can recall and what each reveals and keep doing it repeatedly. As you develop THANKFULNESS into a habit, you will soon find it easier to EMBRACE a loving approach and release guilt, blame, shame, and many other harmful emotions. The treasures you receive when you do are better health, happiness, and a more positive outlook.

Fortunes in Forgiveness

We love to hold onto our stories of the past. They seem so familiar and give us a way to understand recurring events. Our stories taught us lessons of awareness, caution, and adaptability. They, in and of themselves, do not stand in our way of moving forward as much as the meaning and emotions we attach to them. These get many people stuck in victimhood as they live in fear and shame. When this happens, they feel that there is no forgive and forget. They feel sorry, drag the heavy stories with them everywhere, and struggle to put energy toward evolving and new VENTURES. That's exhausting!

Unless you let go of attached negative aspects of your past, you will drain your energy as you lug these stories around with you forever. They will disrupt every aspect of your life, especially your relationships, and trap you in never-ending feelings of hurt, bitterness, and resentment. The pain can get so deep and lasting that some might mask it with addictive gratification activities, like alcohol, drugs, sex, or other dopamine-inducing pleasures. You can imagine what happens when these behaviors persist.

Even the most grateful people can have a tough time being THANKFUL when scorned. We often love and give so generously of ourselves that we unknowingly expect fantasies of perfection to come true. Instead, we experienced disappointment after disappointment. You see, we are all perfectly imperfect. You must be willing to forgive yourself for your shortcomings and others for theirs. As you forgive, you allow the power of THANKS to move you toward a more peaceful life.

Law of Forgiveness - Forgive yourself and others to live a life of freedom from holding onto negative energy.

Forgive Me

Humans want so much to be understood, accepted, and appreciated for who they are. We work so hard to bring out the best in ourselves and set high standards to meet or exceed expectations. Our incentives range from achieving meaningful goals, feelings of belonging, or simply experiencing a rewarding life. We know when we succeed as pride, confidence, love, and other emotions rush through our veins and hearts. It can be so intense that we want to experience it again and again. Sometimes it can even become an obsession.

> ⚡ *Open your mind to lessons from your past to release the pain and forgive yourself. Use your new learning now to create greater ADVENTURES to come.*

On the flip side, when we do not live up to our expected potential, our self-esteem takes a hit. Each one of us has had a lifetime of successes and mistakes. Although we would prefer to remember our accomplishments over our mistakes, we generally hold onto the thoughts and feelings we fixate on most. Our stories are filled with what we wish we woulda, knew we shoulda, and perhaps coulda, but didn't. They also contain actions we should not have done but did. It happens to all of us. Sometimes we brush them off and move on. Depending on the severity of the damage suffered, they may leave physical or emotional scars. These scars are where the stories and all of the attached pain exist. Sadly enough, with great pain, however, comes the deepest learning. When events are not resolved, you will continue to feel the pain that can create a cascade of problems in other areas of your life. The key is forgiveness! To heal, you must address painful experiences, learn from them, and forgive yourself and anyone else involved.

> ⚡ *Let go of your heavy burdens of drama. Use the lessons of your past to create something new with intention, forgive your imperfections, and allow the rest to fade away.*

Each of your stories will affect you the same way as long as you hang onto the meaning you assigned them. You can EMBRACE a more supportive view only when you release your grip and let go of excuses. When you release your hold on past pain, you will lighten up, make space for self-forgiveness, and grow in wisdom.

For example, if you are holding onto the pain from an old relationship, you might find it difficult to commit to or be emotionally invested in a new relationship. The stories of their many faults, your guilt, or maybe even your deep love for them will stay with you and weigh you down. One way to heal is to accept that you are human and forgive yourself for your indiscretions. Keep in mind that apologies do not justify our actions. We are still responsible for what we have done. By forgiving ourselves, we deepen our ability to love, create more peace, and feel more confident about entering into a new relationship. The experience of learning, cleansing, and forgiveness can also invite us to extend THANKS to and improve other close relationships now.

If you are not seeing any value or lessons in your past stories, it may simply be time to release the energy and let them go. In many cases, the reasons we dwelled on them may have seemed silly and reflect our old habitual ways of thinking or acting. When you realize the story no longer serves a purpose, you can decide to let the emotional nonsense go. But do not stop there. Graciously forgive yourself for holding onto it. Almost guaranteed, you will feel a burst of energy, a lightness, and acceptance when you do. It is okay to be perfectly imperfect!

> *Get used to being human. Forgive yourself. When you do not tap into the power of forgiveness, you will struggle to offer the same to others.*

The main idea here is, if you struggle in any relationship, take ownership of your actions and face the good, the bad, and the ugly. Then lighten up and give yourself and others a break. To make amends for your part, use what you have learned, forgive yourself and others, and make better decisions in the future. Others will either come around or fade away.

Forgive Thee

Forgiveness begins with ourselves, but to be freer of heavy negative emotions, we will want to extend the same to others. We all know that forgiving others can be easy for some and difficult for others. The decision is an individual one and usually depends on the extent of who was involved, what happened, and how often it occurred. To forgive someone who upset us, insulted us, belittled us, shamed us, or made us cry can be a bitter pill to swallow. It's even worse when the suffering lasts for a long time or physical harm occurs. We know how many of these situations play out. Sometimes the devastation can leave scars so deep that the traumatic feeling is repeatedly triggered and resurfaces even for the slightest reason. These types of circumstances are devastating and their impact is not to be discounted. With such challenges, forgiveness is normally the last thing on our minds. The point here is to recognize that we all have the choice of holding onto pain or letting it go. The answer lies in knowing the freedom you will experience when you let go of the pain tied to your memories and step into new ADVENTURES with less burdens.

I met a lady who struggled with her veteran husband's service-connected disabilities. He was in a major accident that caused Post Traumatic Stress Disorder (PTSD) and was physically unable to provide selfcare. Although very much in love with his wife, he eventually became very irritable and began treating her harshly. He would make snide remarks about the way she looked, her inability to care for him on her own, and her lack of competence. Yet she was beautiful, compassionate, and intelligent and brought much patience, value, and confidence into the relationship.

This corrosive environment began to impact her personal relationships at home and work. She often thought about throwing in the towel and leaving him but she loved him and knew that would only worsen his issues. She stayed with him for many years and, over time, absorbed his negative energy. Eventually, they realized they were constantly arguing. Through professional guidance, they learned to better understand each other's perspectives and how each felt. Her realization was she had a choice and made the decision to stay. She loved him and wanted the best for him but simply did not know how to do it. His realization was he was depressed due to his inability to be mobile. He also loved her and did not know where to channel his negative energy, except at her, the closest one to him. Together they learned how to improve their ability to lovingly communicate, control their urges to speak harshly, and apologize when they hurt one another. They consistently practiced these simply stated but very challenging strategies and were soon able to speak freely about their needs. With some time and a lot of forgiveness, they healed their marriage.

> *Apologize immediately and sincerely once you realize the faulty part you played. Own it and do not expect the other person to do the same. They must go through their own forgiveness process. Your actions will help you speed up their process of self-forgiveness.*

This story represents a beautiful demonstration of how understanding and learning new skills can lead to forgiveness. It also may sound simple, but forgiveness can be very complex and complicated. To forgive does not mean you're letting people walk all over you. The wisdom you gain from your memories can make you aware of and help you deal with that. At the same time, most people are doing the best they can in their desires to be good. More often than not, their intentions are noble and innocent. If you struggle to see it that way and cannot forgive, maybe your stories are giving you a sense of security - a false sense of steady security. Our desire to not forgive is a ploy to shield or distract us from having to deal with the hurt caused. Forgive does not mean forget, but with one step at a time, you can gradually clear the air and forgive. Ultimately, you must decide whether to hold onto the heavy burden of remorse or forgive and let it go.

> ⚡ *Take one small step toward forgiveness. Just by taking that small step you can learn to release energy tied to grief, fury, and trauma. This will increase your ability to authentically love others, ENJOY life to the fullest, and experience peace.*

Grateful Creations

We often take for granted the life we currently have and the many wonderful things we manifested. We pay little attention to the gifts of love, graciousness, abundance, success, prosperity, and so on. It's like everything just magically appeared and will be there forever. The fact is, we are the creators and the beneficiaries of everything in our surroundings. All that you have is a result of who you have been, how you have been thinking, and what you have done. Although some aspects may be undesirable, they all have their own purpose and value. Otherwise, why would you have it in your life?

Strangely enough, instead of offering THANKS for our creative genius, we seem to focus more on what bothers us, like our imperfections, weaknesses, and errors. We become fixers. There is nothing wrong with making improvements. They are our desire to show that we

> ⚡ *Give THANKS to your lifelong developments. You have been on a path to unfold and use strategies that created who you are today. Through experience and knowledge, you have gained inner wisdom which deserves celebration and appreciation.*

can get or do better or correct something we perceive is broken or not right. We all want to make ourselves and our surroundings better. On the other hand, development is the use of our discoveries, a creative unfolding of our hard-earned wisdom. With a focus on self-development, we experience greater advancements that may include improvements along the way. Take a deep look inside yourself and you will soon discover the abundance and magnificence of the creations you ENJOY today.

My Nature and Personality

Each one of us stands out in our own unique ways. You come with your DANCE, experiences, roles, and many other traits that differ from everybody else. Nobody can do what you can quite like you. If you think about it, you have a lot to be THANKFUL for. The world needs your unique ideas, passions, and aspirations to help it grow and continue to create. When you ask others what they see as the best in you, you may be surprised what comes back. You might feel a bit uncomfortable receiving the compliments at first because you may be blind to your own value or pride yourself on being humble. Knowing your value to others can increase your confidence and motivate you to give more of your best and excel. As for your humbleness, open yourself to gracefully accept the kind words. At the same time, know that you can always grow and continue your self-development. Rest assured, you are appreciated more than you realize. Until you EMBRACE this idea, you will struggle to give THANKS for your unique qualities.

#67 the rose garden – be the observer of your own world. Look from eyes outside of your garden for an objective view of what's going on inside of it.

Another way you can discover your greatness is through the roles you play, such as relationships, friendships, entrepreneurship, citizenships, mentorships, ownerships, fellowships, memberships, sportsmanship, championships, etc. The suffix 'ship', meaning role, is our way of relating to people, things, places, and events. In the many roles you've been playing, consider the favorable feedback you received from people you impacted the most. Also, include the impact the lessons have made from any mistakes. The overall point is not to glorify yourself in your achievements but more for you to appreciate who you have become through your accomplishments. In the end, you will feel more positive and generate a sense of confidence, vitality, and inspiration to enhance your roles and continue to grow.

> *Compile your life's resume. It will offer you insights into how you have been serving the world in a way only you can. That is something to be THANKFUL for!*

People's inability to capture their greatness became quite evident to me as a supervisor. My employees often experience problems writing their self-assessment, a write-up about accomplishments and positive contributions. Their struggle was in capturing their value without feeling like they were bragging. For those who wanted help, I would guide them through their job objectives, what they did, and how their actions aligned with our mission. We would then determine how their work satisfied organizational requirements and goals and any of their innovative solutions. We worked on quantity, timeliness, and completeness. Finally, we would include feedback such as exemplary comments, awards, recognitions, and other positive outcomes to shine a light on their quality work. Through this process, they provided factual input without embellishing the truth or feeling conceited or vain. As they completed the process, they were delighted to see their positive contributions, THANKFUL for the opportunities, and energized to bring higher value to our team.

My Personal Manifestations

With the magic of your inner world, you've been designing your physical surroundings as well. You very likely have some form of shelter, food and water, a physical body, a family or social construct, and modes of energy that are vital to your life and readily available to you. Herein lies your opportunity to offer THANKS for their individual treasures. What does this benefit? Gratitude helps stimulate the NURTURING, loving energy to generate richer relationships. This energy will allow you to tap into your creative potential, enhance what you already have, and develop more of what you want. Invest in THANKING everything that brings you great value just by having it in your world, and watch the magic unfold.

> ⚡ *Make a long list of THANKS for everything big and small in your life. It offers a way to honor and protect your values or ease pain. In doing so, you may find it easier to NURTURE what you value now and get rid of the unwanted when you are ready.*

Many of us give THANKS, say grace, or offer prayers before meals. Some still do that today, and others have stopped for whatever reasons. But this is a perfect example of giving THANKS for what you have. If you think about it, a lot of time, energy, and resources go into making a meal. From the soil to the plate in front of you, the process is laborious and extensive. People tend to forget and take that creation in front of them for granted. We go about our days knowing we will have food, water, and shelter. That is until a catastrophe happens and we lose everything. Disaster extends even beyond Mother Nature's events to our own mistakes, job loss, terminal illness, death of a loved one, and so on. Not only does it affect basic necessities, but it can put a toll on every other part of your life, from heightened tensions, breakdown of a relationship, and declined health.

#35 prayer – no matter how you actively pursue answers to your dilemmas, do so with the clarity, intention, and details of what you want.

My family went through something similar when I was an infant. At that time, my father was a young enlisted Marine and deployed to support war efforts in Vietnam. We didn't have the technology we do today to easily communicate and transfer funds. During that time, my mother did not know how to contact him to let him know she needed money. By using her resourceful talents with what little money she received, Mom did her best to keep us fed, clothed, and sheltered. She diligently kept up the household and, at every meal, gave heart-felt THANKS for the food, family, and home we had. Although she was exhausted, she relied on the small amount of food, plenty of water, and the power of gratitude to keep the family going. When Dad returned home from his deployment, he was shocked at what he found. Despite the kids being healthy, she was skin and bones. He felt so bad and vowed he would do everything in his power to never allow that to happen again. From that point on, Mom thrived in creativity by not having to live in survival mode. She made delicious meals and super cute clothes, mostly from scratch. She NURTURED us and gave THANKS for everything, big and small.

This powerful story is an example of how gratitude can help you keep positive, ENJOY what you have, and NURTURE your relationships, especially with those who give THANKS along with you. If ever you struggle with existing parts of your personal world, then extend THANKS for the treasures you have. What happens afterward can be quite powerful!

My Professional Exhibits

The amount of time we spend at work must bring us some type of value or we wouldn't be doing it. Our professional environments are where many of us spend nearly one-third of our lives and even more if we rob ourselves of personal time and sleep. Be careful, though, not to confuse time with value. Even though you may receive hourly wages, your employers compensate you for the value you bring, not the time you spend behind your desks, in the field, traveling, etc. As an employee, you go to some worksite, interact within the environment, and bring home a paycheck. If you are a business owner, you pay yourself for the effort you put into your work, yet the time you invest in your work is usually longer. And, for homemakers, your occupation frees others to generate monetary income while you ensure the home runs smoothly; your work seems constant. All roles have their advantages and disadvantages!

We often stop appreciating our jobs when we believe it no longer fulfills any of our values. If you find your work does not bring you the value you desire, then it's time to ask why you are there. You may be comparing your income, benefits, or recognition to what other people experience. Professional relationships, organizational politics, or operational inefficiencies may be challenging you. Your boss may be unreasonable, or the work may not be stimulating enough. As your focus continues on your occupational dissatisfaction, you may miss out on the value it brings. Rest assured, these stressful environments exist. The fact is you chose this job, started your business, or stayed a homemaker to fulfill one or more of your values at the beginning. Generally speaking, if you are still doing the work, then it still serves some purpose, or you would have left. Do your best to offer THANKS for that, as it could very well be filling an integral need in your life.

As you depart any unrewarding job, you may wonder about the point of being THANKFUL. Quite frankly, your performance will suffer if you hang onto negative feelings tied to your present work. If you decide to leave, do not burn bridges. They may be the ones you need to cross for a future job. Also, during job hunting efforts, prospective employers may be able to detect unwanted energy behind your undesirable stories. By giving THANKS for the opportunity to work, you release stress, clear up your attitude, and create a more pleasant experience in your present or future jobs. One of the most significant benefits of gratitude is the ease with which you EMBRACE where you are at that moment while searching for what will offer you greater value in your next work ADVENTURE.

I went through quite a few tough times in my professional career. During one painful experience, I was professionally embarrassed and felt like a failure after being removed from a job when the team disbanded. With the complexity involved in removing the entire leadership team, a transition to an unwanted new evaluation rating program, and the chaotic behavior of disgruntled employees, I wanted to throw in the towel. I was on the verge of selling my house, buying an RV, and leaving it all behind. I decided I was not quite ready for that, so I began hunting for my next job. I applied to a wide range of positions above, equal to, and below my expertise and pay grade at that time.

> *Find the value in your employment. It could be money, easy commute, mentally or physically challenging work, flexibility, quiet atmosphere, social connections, etc. If you struggle to find the value, simply be THANKFUL for that discovery and prepare to move on.*

My resume was good, but my energy in my interview skills needed an overhaul. I interviewed for at least 25 jobs in two months and was turned down for every one of them even though I was highly qualified. I had such a heavy heart and desire to be somewhere other than where I was. I knew I had to try something different. After a while, my new boss, Tony, came in. He recognized my passion for leaving yet still asked me to stay. He said that my knowledge was too valuable, and I had strong interpersonal relationships that would support team goals. He asked that I remain long enough to orient him within the organization. Although I didn't stop looking for another job, I jumped on the invitation. I treated it as a chance to learn more about myself and heal. Tony was a solid, kind leader who allowed me to grow with more leadership opportunities and meaningful work. To strengthen our working relationship, we would even head down to the cafeteria in the mornings and eat grits and eggs at the start of our day. I ENJOYED his leadership and worked hard for him.

I often revisited the painful experiences of my former job and soon came to grips with what happened. I recognized the complexity and the roles each of us played and pulled out the lessons. As I did, I felt peace by giving THANKS for the opportunity to experience those tough challenges that helped me grow. I also showed appreciation for my friends and coworkers, who stood by me the entire time. Before leaving, I publicly THANKED Tony for recognizing my potential and offering me a gracious space to heal through compassion and acceptance. From there, I knew better things would follow, and they did. In my follow-on leadership roles, I taught others the many lessons I learned through coaching and mentorship and displayed RESILIENCE in challenging jobs. I also created a coaching and consulting business to help others lead themselves and their teams through difficult situations.

A Future to Appreciate

Since the past created our current circumstances, what is happening now will affect the future in some way! If we accept this idea in its truest sense, we would consciously make choices that shape tomorrow. The funny thing is, we generally do not. Instead, we continue thinking, feeling, and doing what the past initially taught us. While in some areas that may help, it falls short in others that require change. Your health, relationships, lifestyle, and wealth continue to be the same because you think and feel the same way about them, and your actions reflect that.

> ⚡ *Express THANKS for what you want. Offering THANKS for the future helps keep you focused, purposeful, and empowered to reach your objectives.*

One of the challenges we experience in making changes for our future is our habits, rituals, and addictions. We've covered that a few times. Another challenge is that we don't ask for what we really want or don't ask correctly. For example, if you ask for more strength, patience, and tolerance, you will receive events that support your desire for strength, patience, and tolerance. That sounds like more hardship is coming your way. Let's say instead, you ask for loving, caring relationships. You can then create strong, patient, and tolerant strategies and express gratitude for those treasures.

> ⚡ *Be careful and specific in what you ask for. Ask for money, and you may receive a penny. Ask for a break, and all of your activities may come to a screeching halt. Know for certain what you want and ask wisely!*

To manifest a desire into your current reality, use create a vision of what you want in your mind. Be specific in what you want and engage all of your senses as if you already have it. Express THANKS for receiving it, and keep your eyes open without an attachment of when and where it will appear. When the time is right, it will appear!

Law of Manifestation - Our thoughts and ideas create things. What we want or do not want, we will bring into our lives.

Wild Imagination

We all have wild imaginations. It is a major influencing factor for what we do, think about, and create. The beauty of our imagination is it's entirely individual. Nobody has the same kind of imagination like you. Our imaginations have been studied, described, and categorized, and their power still fascinates scientists and other experts. Most scientists theorize that our imagination is a huge factor that sets us apart from other animals. We can create images and run realistic scenarios in our brains that feed our intuition. What's more, we can bring into being what we imagine. That is only the beginning!

> ⚡ *Use your imaginative power to its fullest. The first step in setting up your future is clearly describing it with all of your senses.*

Nothing created came to be without a mental image or idea of what could be. Or a better way to say it is, everything created by humans was first imagined. Your imagination can become a powerhouse when you add emotion and act out the images as if they already exist!

Law of Imaging - We must use our imagination to manifest what we desire.

Feel it

The power of our minds is immense. We think things into existence all of the time without even knowing it. Yet, manifestation remains mysterious to many of us in how it all works. Although we recognize that having a clearly imagined experience plays an important part, other aspects will help it come to fruition. This is where your emotions come into play.

Along with the outer feeling of touch, imagine what emotions you will experience when you have it. Drum up those feelings of joy, happiness, and above all, gratitude. Here is where the power comes into play! Dr. Joe Dispenza proves this in his workshops and addresses it in his book, *Becoming Supernatural: How Common People Are Doing the Uncommon.* He states that gratitude is the ultimate state of receivership. The feelings of having what you want are significantly enhanced by the THANKFUL feelings you send as if you already have it. In other words, generate a sense of gratitude you will experience when you receive it before physically possessing it. Have faith in your belief that it will eventually appear and allow the surprise to happen.

> *Keep faith in knowing you will receive your future desires. Doubts throw you off and distract you from receivership. You have a role to play in receiving. Part of that role is being THANKFUL and open to receive!*

Intuitive Powers

Our imagination, faith, and gratitude will be less effective if unwilling to take the action necessary to bring what we desire into our lives. We have to know the places our desires may appear and yet not expect them. Sometimes we find them in the oddest places, and they are often right in our path. Here is where you harness the power of your intuition. The word 'tuition' in its origin means to look after or be the guardian of. You develop your 'intuition' based on what you know to be true for yourself. They are your instincts or what you know to be true without a full reasoning process. You can only acquire and strengthen the function of your intuition through your own experiences.

Undoubtedly on many occasions, we can be grateful for our intuition. It has incredible power, but only if you learn to trust and use it. Each of us has used intuition in the past, with varying results. Many still struggle to use it effectively. To do so wisely, consider the upsides and downsides of what will happen when you apply what it's telling you. There is risk in everything, and knowing the threats in advance will help ensure success. With practice, you will develop more powerful, intuitive senses and make choices with faith and less doubt.

For those who have read *The Secret of the Ages* by Robert Collier, you know the secret to the Law of Attraction is through thought, feeling, and action. You have the power to attract it, but if you don't know what you're looking for, you'll miss it. If you don't dare to seek it, you'll lessen your chances of finding it. If you don't trust your intuition and take the initiative to receive it, it may never be realized.

Law of Attraction - Where your attention goes, energy flows. You will attract into your life what you focus your attention on most.

We have so much to be THANKFUL for in our lives. Pay attention to the goodness and opportunity that surrounds you. Your many decisions with people, places, things, and events of your past have brought you where you are today. You have the power of freedom to choose whether to hold on to them or let go. Your present creations continue to offer limitless possibilities to develop a future you love. It is up to each one of us to know what we want so we create our favorite ADVENTURE. Stop living in the past, and do not wait for the future to come. Bring the future to your present and start behaving like it is already here. Dream it, feel it, and express THANKS for it. Have faith in your powerful mind, courageous abilities, and ongoing initiative, and watch your visions magically appear, just like you asked.

> *Elevate your feelings of gratitude toward your imagined outcome. As you keep your faith, you will let go of frustration and watch it materialize.*

UPLIFT

W e live in a beautiful world full of unique people, places, things, and events. It offers us many reference points to gauge how we want to live. We make comparisons and judgments to assess where we are, what it will take to be successful, and the many ways to reach our goals. Along the way, some people encourage us, while others express their fears. In response, we either EMBRACE their optimism or suppress our true desires. Either way, we sometimes struggle with feeling like we belong. This feeling can put a damper on our ability to pursue lofty goals, move from one ADVENTURE to the next, and create suitable lives. If this sounds like you, you are not alone. All of us go through similar challenges and hardships at some point in our lives, but that does not mean that any one of us is superior or inferior to another.

The truth is, we are all on individual journeys, moving at our own pace, and doing the best we can with what we have. When you view people as greater or less than you, catch yourself and recognize that they are at a different stage of their own ADVENTURE. Through this more neutral view, you can confidently choose what is best for you and leave lopsided judgment behind. Any heavy one-sided judgments and comparisons of yourself, others, and different societies reveal your sense of insecurity about you and your life. To UPLIFT yourself and everyone or everything around you, see everyone as equal. They have their greatness and faults and you have yours. If you are constantly seeing negative, start looking for the positive. If you continue to see their great attributes, just know that they struggle with their own issues.

> *Balance your idea of greatness. You will take the focus off of what others own and achieve so you can decide more objectively what fits into your lifestyle.*

We all have them. Through a balanced approach, you can handle situations more objectively and confidently, UPLIFT yourself, and pull others up with you.

Reflections of You

Everything in your world directly reflects who you believe you are. The people, things, and activities around you are what you see in the mirror. The good and bad, along with right and wrong, are also reflections of your perceptions and reality. We cast judgments on ourselves to fit our self-imposed standards. We compare ourselves to others to keep improving or developing. These beliefs are normal and natural, but they can also throw you off balance and move you away from your purpose if not tempered.

Check your honesty by looking in the mirror and assessing what you see. An honest assessment will unveil the current struggles between your values and what you say and do. We want to live our truth, show up authentically, and be our best. When you look in the mirror, you have the power of choice to EMBRACE aspects about yourself or change the undesirable ones. Just remember, you will remain in conflict with yourself and others if you do not focus your energy on your values.

> *Evaluate who you say you are to be on equal footing with others. Otherwise, you will live in conflict within yourself. You may escape others, but you will never get away from yourself.*

Mirror, Mirror

Our society paints images of aesthetically pleasing models with perceived perfect bodies, flawless faces, and manicured fingernails. They seem to ENJOY the ideal life with fancy things and loving relationships. This untrue commercialized fallacy influences our perceptions of perfection and success. We put these picture-perfect ideals on high pedestals and feel bad for not being, doing, or having what others have. Our inner critic has a heyday with these feelings and wreaks havoc on our self-image. We unrealistically begin to want every bit of what they have right now. The stress creates anxiety as we desperately seek unrealistic, commercialized goals. By hook or crook, we vow to ourselves to fix it all! And companies will continue to sell you a vast array of goods and services to reach this unattainable perfection.

> *Uncover your beauty. We all have parts about ourselves that we do not like, but your beauty lies in the unique qualities that set you apart. EMBRACE them, and you will soon see yourself in a different, more positive light.*

Law of Reflection - What you see in others, you see in yourself, whether you like it or not.

A friend of mine was so obsessed with having the perfect body that she went to great lengths to get it. Although Jane was not a large woman, she underwent medical procedures to remove fat cells and tighten her skin all over her body. Whenever she saw a jiggle or extra skin, she saw herself as fat. Her flaws became even more disturbing to her when she became pregnant with her second child. A short time after the birth of her child, Jane had one surgery after another. She ended up tens of thousands of dollars in debt and complained that she looked like a patch quilt doll. Her turning point was when her children began to talk and pointed out her scars. She told them enough to satisfy their curiosity and left it there. Her children's comments sparked deeper questions not only about Jane herself but also about her children's future self-esteem and body image. Jane finally called it quits and eventually learned to EMBRACE her perceived flaws. Sometimes it takes a lot for people to see their natural beauty.

Your perceptions of how you see yourself can affect every aspect of your life if you let it. For most of us, when we see our reflections, our focus will often go right to our flaws. It is normal for us to want to improve but destructive when all we see is our imperfections. The impact goes well beyond mere vanity and can affect our health, longevity, and happiness. Most of us know this, yet we keep running on this endless hamster wheel. When you have fixated enough on your flaws and are ready to feel better about yourself, shift your focus to aspects about yourself that you like. Each of us has unique, beautiful traits to UPLIFT.

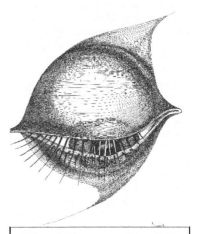

#59 angel fish – we are all beautiful in unique ways. When you look through your own eyes and find your beauty, you will begin to notice it everywhere!

Pick out your unique qualities and start focusing on them. If you cannot see them, others can. Consider the qualities about yourself that others have mentioned in the past, or ask them. Over time your shifted focus will release the anxiety and depression of failing to live up to some imagined or commercialized standard. You get to decide who you want to be, how you want to look, and what you want in your life. If you have traits you'd like to change for whatever reason, you can either VENTURE to change them or EMBRACE them and celebrate your uniqueness. Remember, as you do, send love to the area you wish to improve and continue to focus on your beauty. In turn, you will lower your stress and increase your creativity to achieve what you want. You are more beautiful than you think!

Law of Self-worth – You can only attract what you feel you are worth. You are not what you have or what you do. The reality is that the more you like yourself, the more others will like you.

Manage Your Inner Critic

Most of us are our own worst critics and are quick to pick out what is wrong with ourselves. Although we all have flaws, that certainly does not stop us from wanting to be seen and heard. Most of us want to do exciting, challenging, and unique things beyond our everyday lives. When all of this comes to a halt, it is mainly because of the little voice in our heads. Our view of ourselves is where our inner critic comes into play.

Your inner critic does its job of pointing out your flaws every day. It focuses on what you do not like and does its best to make you feel less than. Your criteria are based on what you believe to be true from what you see, hear, and feel. Your perception generally created a baseline of how you see yourself now and what you will create in the future. This scrutiny applies to every personal and professional area of your life. Setting standards is not a bad thing. Your inner critic basically keeps you in check with your standards or truths. As you focus on those set standards, you will naturally strive to achieve them. The problems occur when your inner critic takes over your sense of reasoning and worth. Its messages can be brutal and direct. It takes practice to control any negative effects it may have on you.

Manage your inner critic. It will grow deafening if you feed it, so do not let it take over. Neutralize it by seeing the good in the bad and bad in the good. When you do so, you will reduce stress, learn to love yourself better, and make more reasonable decisions.

Some people say not to listen to the inner critic. Quite frankly, it simply needs to be tamed, understood, and appreciated. It wants you to feel accepted, admired, and celebrated versus rejected, humiliated, and unappreciated. When properly controlled, any frustration behind your inner critic can drive you to make changes you know are necessary. You can do this by examining its messages to determine if they are loving and align with your values. Although your values can inspire you to take action, ensure you have a balanced perspective in your approach. With a new outlook, you will release pressure and tackle change realistically and more creatively.

Critics on the Outside

We have a lot of noise going on inside of our heads. It's a wonder we can hear anything else, but we do, even when we don't want to. Many of our thoughts about ourselves stem from what other people experience with us. People love to offer their opinions, but you can also learn a lot from their nonverbal gestures. All of this feedback equips your inner critic. With it, you form perceptions of what is acceptable or unacceptable. This decision then creates your own beliefs and truths and helps you establish your standards. We all do this. Although the criticism can be constructive, it also can be disruptive. You can either enable it to UPLIFT you or drag you down. If you want to lift yourself from the noise, focus on the positive aspects of their feedback and consider the negative. Both negative and positive feedback have the ability to UPLIFT us.

I had a hay day with my inner critic as a teenager as I was going through puberty. One summer, I unwittingly indulged in a high carb diet that led to a significant weight gain. In the most compassionate way possible, my family and friends did their best to let me know what they saw. I also picked up the same type of vibes from those who said nothing. The thing was, I already knew I had put on some pounds and felt embarrassed by their remarks. I

> *Be you. Accept from others only what you feel is valid for you. Because you may not see yourself as others do, consider and evaluate their feedback. Use what is helpful, and UPLIFT yourself by knowing you are making progress.*

was too young to know what to do. My mother picked up on my disappointment and asked if I wanted to go to the "spa" and exercise with her.

The transformation that ensued led to a lifetime path of health and fitness. From that point on, I played volleyball, ran track, participated in bodybuilding and weight lifting contests, completed numerous marathons and other races, hiked many trails, and rode hundreds of bike miles. I also taught aerobics, personally trained both men and women, coached cross country and track, and most of all withstood the vigorous Marine Corps physical requirements. I took to heart what the earlier outer critics were saying and kicked myself into action. Again, it's not about what is said. It's about how true the feedback is for you and what you do with it.

So many of us grew up with the guidance to be humble, modest, and not brag. We downplay our beauty, intellect, and talents so we do not offend others who may feel envious or resentful. We joke about ourselves, so we mask our strengths and personal power. These words and ideas are self-destructive. To be humble and modest does not mean ignoring your qualities and values. A better approach is for you not to exaggerate your abilities and EMBRACE that other people are just as good in various areas of life, if not better than you. They are working from their heart and with intention. In his book

> *Receive compliments openly. They are gifts and beneficial to both the giver and receiver. By opening your arms to receive compliments, you deepen your self-love and tame your inner critic.*

Speed of Trust, Stephen Covey states, "Being humble doesn't mean being weak, reticent, or self-effacing. It means recognizing principles and putting it ahead of self. It means standing firmly for principle, even in the face of opposition." You simply need to dig deeper inside to gain answers to challenging areas if you want something better or different. People who sit on their achievements and do not improve will soon become irrelevant. Acknowledge your areas of greatness and continue to develop them. At the same time, consider other new VENTURES. In this way, you will keep your inner critic in check. Your beautiful and unique traits, intellect, and talents are treasures to be UPLIFTED and celebrated. EMBRACE and be proud of them!

Law of Identity - We are what we say we are and that which we accept others of saying.

Criticism of Errors

Our shortcomings can certainly drag us down. We often beat ourselves up for even the most minor mistakes. Our mistakes create a feast for our inner critic and stick with us until we learn from them and decide to let them go. The thing is, you are human and err. The only thing you can do to heal is take ownership of your mistake, apologize to yourself and others you hurt, and forgive. You do the best you can with what you know, what you have, and what you're willing to do at that moment. Most of the time, your indiscretions are impulsive behaviors that point to some unresolved event in your past. This memory stays with you and, even as you own up to your mistakes, will continue to wreak havoc on your ability to make wise decisions. The more mistakes you make that align with this past event, the less peace, joy, and happiness you'll have in your world. It's hard to feel good about ourselves when we realize the error in our ways. By knowing we have the power to change, we can UPLIFT ourselves from these mistakes. That takes reason and self-love.

Law of Dissonance – You live in self-delusion and create mental tension when a belief or thought does not align with your actions. You can reduce them by changing a belief or action.

As you work through your blunders, recognize that reasoning does not justify your actions, nor does self-love justify indifference to everyone else. Consider your impact on others and how it affected them. Sometimes even actions that are not directed at a person can have negative effects. As a simple example, let's say you swiped salt and pepper shakers from a restaurant. Your reason may be that you thought they were unique and wanted a souvenir. As you walk out, the host discretely calls you out and asks you to

> *Lighten your heavy energy to UPLIFT yourself. As you find the uniqueness in your DANCE and release the standards of perfection, you can open the path for others to do the same.*

leave them behind. With attitude in hand, you slam them down in an angry fit and leave. The host places the items back on the table and is finished with the issue. Embarrassed because you've been caught, you hang onto the story and feelings and decide never to go there again. There is a lot to unpack here, and most of us can see the many errors. The first was your choice to steal. This decision not only impacted your image but also the restaurant's staff in their ability to trust customers. Another was your choice to not own up to your indiscretions, respectfully hand the shakers back, and apologize.

Whenever you are left holding the bag of negative shame energy for yourself, whether major or minor, own up to it, apologize, offload that energy, and open yourself to self-forgiveness and self-love. You will feel a sense of lightness that makes it easier to UPLIFT yourself. When you finally realize you are perfectly imperfect, just like everyone else, you will stop blaming, shaming, and regretting and begin to EMBRACE your humanness, deepen your learning, and ENJOY life. Although some people may choose not to accept your apology, it is their choice to continue to hold onto the negative energy. Wish them well. As you do, it extends the invitation for them to do the same and UPLIFT themselves later on.

Here Comes the Judge

We try so hard not to judge others, but we often fall into that trap. Most of the time, we judge and compare to make decisions for ourselves because we need a baseline from which to choose. Other times, our judging is due to a discomfort with ourselves or cultural ways we learned during formative years and beyond. We drum up prior decisions, rely on old thought processes, and lean on beliefs and attitudes. Over time, we unintentionally create habits of thinking everyone should be the same and conform to us. Naturally, in an attempt to make sense of what we do not understand, we initially may trigger our survival lizard brains. But we need to move consciously beyond these situations. Unfortunately, many of us will react with attitudes based on immediate perceptions. Our prejudging is where we lose focus of how we see ourselves and shift our attention toward how we see them. This shift is only helpful if we view their differences in a loving manner and EMBRACE them as a part of our deeper learning.

The key to unlocking our ability to UPLIFT each other is to take the time to better understand and respect the wide variety of people and the unique ADVENTURES they are on. Michio Kaku, professor of physics at the City University of New York and best-selling author writes that "A young child, born in one culture can easily grow up and mature in another totally different culture, even if the two cultures may be separated by a vast cultural chasm." You may not be able to recognize similarities if you do not experience them for yourself in some way. When you look at other people, cultures, and countries, you will soon realize that although different, we share common basic needs for safety, understanding, love, connection, freedom, and creation. We simply go about life differently because we come from our own habits, perspectives, and attitudes.

Law of Polarity – Everything has an opposite that validates our choices. Forces come in pairs: masculine/feminine, action/reaction, negative/positive. Nothing exists alone!

Deep Rooted Outlooks

If you ever want an unfiltered view about something, ask little kids. They can tell or draw for you what they notice. When you ask what Grandma looks like, they may describe her very well but not have an extensive framework to judge what they see. To them, everything is basic. Almost everybody is tall, and some people are larger than others, but none receive labels until children learn them. They also can make comparisons to other characters in their world, such as people with very long necks and giraffes. When they establish their reference points, they will not hesitate to blurt out a label, a comparison, or an unanticipated question to gain a better understand. It is quick, to the point, and gets them back to playtime. Gradually, as they receive feedback, they learn how to filter their words about what they see to improve social interactions. They know through various established standards, most of which are labels, how to describe others.

> *Reject labels. Stick to the descriptive facts and work from there. Once you make any label your truth, you may struggle with your willingness to let it go.*

With that in mind, it's easy to see how we create perceptions through comparisons and judging others. We point the finger and judge because we do not open our minds to understand others better and what they are dragging around with them. Quite frankly, what you see in them directly reflects what you would see in yourself if you were in their shoes. You will feel their pain or their joy. We all have our stories, and our physical, mental, and emotional scars remind us of them. These perceptions can be in any area of our lives, including wealth, health, intellect, lifestyle, friendships, and many others. To UPLIFT others, we need to EMBRACE our current understanding of where they are and where they want to be, not what we assume to be true or best for them. You can UPLIFT any person through kindness, respect, love, and peace. That's where it all begins!

Law of Grace – Share what you have been given with mercy, love, and willingness, and you shall also receive the same.

Social Perspectives

The old English proverb, "birds of a feather flock together," is so true for us in many ways. We often identify with people similar to us in age, sex, race, religion, lifestyle, professions, and other observable similarities. Groups of people do not stop there, though. Other characteristics that attract people to one another include personality, energy, activity levels, intellect, values, etc. It's easy for people in those groups to connect as most share the same experiences or views. Unless we are open or spend enough time to understand the people in the group, we will tend to discriminate through stereotypes and prejudices. Quite frankly, most of us want to know why people say and do things differently. It's in our natural makeup to explore and reason, but many of us are too unmotivated to invest our time. Sadly, if we are not truly part of the group, we get the information through multiple sensationalized media outlets and other people's views to form our judgments. We lack understanding of every group we are not a part of; no one is immune. First-hand experiences and solid research are the only ways to understand, and even then, you are only aware of what you observe and interpret through your own experiences.

#12 saturday evening post – the many media outlets will do their best to seduce you and pull you into their sensationalist ways. Don't give them your energy, lest they rob you of your joy and peace!

Whether you are in the group or not, you'll form your opinions. All communities have issues, and they also have a lot of goodness in them. To objectively appreciate their value, it would be necessary to see both. As you get to know their upsides and downsides, you'll be able to maintain a more balanced approach to the benefits they bring and the challenges they pose. These are the areas you can UPLIFT to foster growth. The benefits are effortless to UPLIFT as they are positive and encouraging. The challenges can be more complex and must be handled gently with care and consideration. If threatened, these fragile parts can create chaos and damage the group's image and progress. When you UPLIFT these groups through balanced compassion and respect, the confusion will simmer down, and peace will ensue. Through research and interactions with multiple group members, you'll better understand their challenges and uncover new truths to create a healthy connection. You might even be surprised at how varied groups are actually very similar to one another.

On the opposite side of the coin, Geoffrey Chaucer, the author best known for *The Canterbury Tales*, used the phrase "Familiarity breeds contempt" in his work, *Tale of Melibee* (c. 1386). Here, Chaucer states that the more familiar we are with people, the higher the chance of losing respect for them over time. Chaucer used this in reference to a person, such as a spouse or close associate. We can apply the same concept to groups we outgrow. Sometimes when you are with a group long enough, resentments, disagreements, and misunderstandings may form. This situation may easily lead you to leave the group discontentedly. As you can imagine, the focus then becomes on the negative aspects that justified the departure instead of the benefits it offered up to that point. Quite often, those benefits don't go away for other people who continue to ENJOY or need them. They simply are outweighed by the unpleasant circumstances you experienced. A situation similar to this happened to me in the Marine Corps and was one of a few reasons I decided to retire after 20 years.

> *Respect groups even as you move on. Just because you no longer are a member does not mean that other people will not benefit from the same experience, especially as they can learn from it. UPLIFT the group's positive qualities and choose to view any shortfalls as footnotes to your history.*

During my last term in the Corps, unbeknownst to me, orders came through for me to move to another duty station. Although I was expecting orders, I wasn't expecting them to occur without a conversation. When the orders finally made it to me after being in the administrative office for over three weeks, I was shocked to discover the short timeframe I would have to sell my home, pack up, and get settled in a new location. A couple of months prior, I had been placed in the selection zone for promotion and anticipated that I would be selected. The conflict between the stress of relocating so quickly and the excitement of the promotion prospect weighed heavy on me. I had to decide whether to accept the orders and receive the promotion or decline both and retire. The decision was a tough one as I ENJOYED my time in the Marine Corps. I also valued my family and understood the personal disruption the move would cause. After a few days, I made my decision to retire. At first, I was still mad about the orders being sent without any conversation in advance. I was also frustrated about the timeframe, yet less about the location.

My decision to balance my emotions about the orders helped me focus on the many qualities I appreciated about the Marine Corps. The Corps offered me opportunities I would not have had otherwise. It was the ADVENTURE of a lifetime that I will never forget. I could have left as a disgruntled service member still hanging onto blame, but I valued the 20 years of my life I committed to serve our country. I have a special place in my heart for the Marine Corps and the dedication, motivation, and love each Marine gives to defending our freedom and rights. Their duty and sacrifice should be recognized and UPLIFTED by all!

If travel is on your ADVENTURE list, be aware of your deep-rooted criticisms and social perspectives. Most of us lay claim to some country or other as our home base. When it comes to how we view other places, we often use our residences as baselines for comparison. Be aware of your perceptions about where you live and what you find UPLIFTING. Also, investigate the location you want to visit so you can make informed and intentional decisions and choose experiences that UPLIFT you and others.

> ✒ *Find distinctive beauty in places you encounter. While every area is different, you remain the same. By honing in on beauty and maintaining awareness of the rest, it will create an UPLIFTING and ENJOYABLE experience.*

For example, if you are visiting Singapore, you will not want to chew gum unless medically prescribed, or you will be fined and possibly jailed. It might sound quirky and restricting to you, but to the citizens in that country it poses health risks and damages the environment. Awareness will help you manage expectations of other countries and their cultures. Let go of high or low expectations and be open to experiencing the people, culture, sights, and sounds. EMBRACE the differences and visit with a sense of intrigue and fascination. As you experience the beauty and value each place offers, you raise your energy and expand your positive energy to UPLIFT those you will meet along the way. By UPLIFTING everyone else, it is easier to focus on unique and exciting ADVENTURES and create an experience you can ENJOY.

A friend of mine hosted his cousin from Europe who wanted to tour the big cities on the east coast of the United States. As his cousin began her tour, he noticed that she constantly complained. She commented negatively about the flimsy houses, litter-filled streets, and restaurant food and service. Although her remarks were accurate, they were taking the wind out of his sails. He decided to chalk them up to her being exhausted from the flight and did his best to let it go. The next day, they headed to Washington, D.C., to explore the monuments and her complaints continued. As they traveled around D.C., her focus seemed to shift a bit from her initial off-putting experiences to the spectacular size and details of all the statues and the museums. When they made their way to New York City, he noticed that she began to praise the sites instead of complaining about unattractive ones. She was spellbound by the liveliness and enormity of the city's structures, statues, and art. Finally, while in Niagara Falls, she was left in awe by the powerful, overwhelming sights and sounds of the waterfalls. As they returned to his house, they chatted about the captivating sites and experiences without one complaint. Through her UPLIFTING, positive experiences and comments, they were able to ENJOY the visit and create memories she would cherish forever. When we open our minds to the idea that people live differently and each place has its qualities, we'll learn to relax, EMBRACE what we see, and ENJOY ourselves. Sometimes it is difficult to truly understand the beauty in a place to UPLIFT it until you actually experience it.

Chapter 9

RESILIENT

*I*t's fascinating to see people accomplish extraordinary feats, especially when they overcome challenging odds that seem to stand in the way. They may have some doubts, but they intuitively know they could do it. They recognize obstacles may arise, yet they seem to conquer them as if they did not exist. They can stay flexible and seize opportunities as they maintain discipline and determination in their quest.

Most of these folks are just like you and me. They are everyday people experiencing success in performing the uncommon. This statement is not to take away from or downplay their struggles. What makes them stand out is their willpower and the tools that keep them RESILIENT through extreme adversity. But think about it. All of us have experienced successes in our lives, big and small. Sometimes, we just do not give ourselves enough credit. Instead, we focus too much on disappointments and not enough on the many challenges we overcome along with the lessons they offer for future success. We quit many activities mostly because they don't align with our values or inspire us. Our failures often come from not acting on our lessons or using the powerful resources we have at our fingertips. We become frustrated, confused, and discouraged as we get wrapped up in our desire to finish instead of ENJOYING the process, learning, and growth along the way.

Commit or Quit

People often cling to things they know they should abandon but refuse to change. They also stop doing things that they know they should continue. Oddly enough, we have all done both, like leaving behind unhealthy eating habits, toxic relationships, excessive alcohol, smoking, procrastinating, cussing, and the list goes on. Our challenge is to know the difference between what is working well and what is not so we can commit or quit. Sometimes we can be so focused on external gratification that when we finally make the decision to quit, it is generally because some force pushed us to do it. If it's not a diagnosis or fear of a fatal disease that pushed us, it could be if we were ridiculed, blamed, or shamed. The question still remains on what is worth our time and effort to continue.

I've known many people who broke difficult habits. Smoking cigarettes seems to be one of the most problematic. Out of curiosity, I reached out to my brother to learn how he quit smoking. He said it didn't just happen overnight. You see, Rob had quit once before but fell back into the habit. He found he was still smoking even when using the nicotine patches. Rob realized he was going to have to do something different if he was going to quit forever, so he started over. As he looked at his daily routine, he noticed his triggers that enticed him to smoke. The biggest trigger was his visits with friends at the smoke pit. Rob let his buddies know that he was giving the pit a break until he no longer felt the desire to smoke around them. He stayed the course and over six months successfully quit smoking. Through awareness, willpower, and altered actions, Rob overcame his own triggers and peer pressure. He kicked the habit and has been smoke-free ever since!

RESILIENCE is about hanging in there for self-discovery and decision-making. Even if you jump into your VENTURE, by learning through self-awareness, knowledge, resources, and intuition, you will better know whether you made the best choice or to change. You will also see strong evidence to support your best decisions if they align with your values. A cautionary note, RESILIENCE and obsession are not the same things. Obsession is about blindly fighting and forcing your way through something in a state of neediness and deprivation. People obsess over things mostly because they lack control over something they may lose. Once they realize they can live without it or have everything they need, they will release their attachment and obsession and end up altering their path. Through RESILIENCE, your grip on the outcome is not as intense, and your approach is more flexible so you can allow yourself time to make adjustments.

Aligning With Your Values

Many folks start new VENTURES like New Year's resolutions, home projects, self-help programs, diets, budgets, and other activities without clarity of a driving force. It's fun and exciting to start new professions, hobbies, or lives together. We feel happy and have a sense of acceptance from others. When we realize it is not what we truly wanted, what may have started as bliss turns into a struggle. We may want to quit but are overpowered by the guilt and remorse connected to losing time or how others will judge us. Most of us do not typically start anything with the intent to quit, although we reserve the right to do so. Yet, even as we try to reason through it, we cannot seem to find the incentive or benefits of sticking with our VENTURE. What we thought would be forever ends up being never more. That is when the conflict within ourselves becomes real, and we start looking elsewhere or for a way out. Before abandoning your ADVENTURE, take a moment and determine if you aligned the event to any one or more of your core values. This step may be the saving grace to keep you RESILIENT.

In AWAKEN, we discussed values and our desires to honor and protect them. You will know whether you value something by the amount of thought, time, and energy you put into it. Most of the time, you will even make excuses to bring things that honor your values into your life. You will not procrastinate to do so or have to be nudged. And you will find it easy to say no to other people, things, or events that attempt to pull you away from them. Your values will also become apparent when you have no problems EMBRACING the various challenges they may bring. You can stay strong and press on by knowing you will benefit from it in the long run. Their internal and external rewards drive hard-working people to overcome struggles every day. What sets them apart from others is the alignment with their values that helps them tap into their RESILIENCE.

Look at what sailors do when they traverse the seas. They value the experience and the joy of being out in the ocean. They learn to navigate the ship with the least damage possible during turbulent waters and go back out again. Their success does not happen with one trip. They love the voyage to the extent that it will always be worth the effort to learn, grow, and master despite the dangers. Without knowing the value and joy in what they do, they probably would not do it. It's a tough job and, to them, meaningful work. They do not wonder if the boat, crew, or supplies are ready. They prepare them and consider the weather and other factors for when challenges arise. You are the sailor of your ship. The wind will blow, and the seas will rock your boat. Remember the statement from Roosevelt in EMBRACE. Not everything will go as you expect, and you will grow beyond your challenges. Through your preparedness, knowing where you want to land, and steering your rudder and sails in that direction, you will navigate the seas and discover ADVENTURES that you have never before experienced.

Law of Commitment - Through clarity, everything manifests easily as long as it is in harmony with your purpose and the universe. That is when indecisiveness seems to fade away.

To some, these concepts may sound too easy and fantasy-like. Many of us value our health, relationships, and money yet continue unhealthy habits, remain alone, and feel deprived. That being the case, it is not your values as much as the beliefs that stand in your way. Think back to a moment when you were doing something important. You did not get distracted, waiver between different things, or make excuses to prolong doing it. You believed what you were doing was a valuable use of your time. You were RESILIENT and overcame obstacles and challenges along your path. With that in mind, take a look back and consider how your ADVENTURE aligned with your values and beliefs.

Now consider an important activity where you struggled. You may have been determined and wanted so much to finish, but things kept pulling you away from your goal. Take a step back and consider your beliefs around the value you expected it to bring. They may be key limiting factors in your ability to focus and commit to the ADVENTURE. If so, you can decide on different beliefs and test them to see which ones will work. This problem occurs quite often in our lives, but we see it mostly with New Year's resolutions and health regimens.

Let's run through a few limiting beliefs around the value of money that many new business owners may experience. Generally speaking, the difference between a business and a hobby is income. While both satisfy a value and can be ENJOYABLE, hobbies are not businesses as, essentially, their intent is not to generate profitable revenue. In a business, you must ask for funds according to the amount appropriate to pay for your work, operate your business, and grow your company. This step is where many struggling business owners stumble because they don't know how much money to ask for or are afraid to ask. They may subconsciously believe that the potential customers will not see the value in the service or product. They may also think that asking for money is rude, rejection is bad, or some other underlying belief. If business owners struggle to produce income, the business will remain or turn into a hobby. As a result, they may experience undesirable feedback unless they change their beliefs and begin asking for suitable pay. For them to change these underlying beliefs will take time and effort, but as they do, it will be easier to stay the course.

Law of Success – With clarity of intention, flow, and passion you will indeed succeed.

Shifting Your Values

Life changes, and as it does, so do our values. Many of us have outgrown specific people, things, and events that were once important to us. As you evolve, so must they, or you will get stuck in your muck. No matter what, your circumstances will undoubtedly change. We can easily see this in situations we've outgrown. For example, we may have valued social activities and games with friends when we were single or intermingling with couples. As our families grew, our values will shift from socialization to more family-focused events. In our professions, we may initially value financial security and later shift our values to ENJOYABLE work over money.

Even when things are going well, sometimes we can suddenly be kicked off course onto another ADVENTURE. This change in direction may point to a conflict in some of your values. We can resolve our conflicting values by realizing which ones offer us the most significant benefit now and over the long haul. This is reprioritization can satisfy a pressing desire where either way you'll benefit. For instance, let's say you value education and work. As you plan to go to college, the job of a lifetime may arise. You might decide to postpone school and take the job to satisfy an immediate need, like income, at that moment. After being on the job, you can honor your value of education by learning on the job and later through continued schooling. You can also benefit by reprioritizing your values in reverse order. Maybe you were offered the job, but you knew education would open more or better opportunities in the future. You can continue schooling and pursue an income-producing profession through internships, part-time jobs, or after you complete training. Both value-shifting approaches can provide lifelong benefits and learning. By carefully considering your values and immediate goals, you will quickly determine the best option. This awareness happened with me a few times and is one of the many reasons I joined the Marine Corps before finishing college.

During my first year of college, I experienced value conflicts between fun and building on a profession through advanced schooling. After the first semester, I soon found myself scattered, stressed, and unfocused. When summer came, I was getting nowhere and knew I needed structure, discipline, and fulfilling work. After much painful reflection, that's when I reprioritized my fun, education, and vocation values and decided to join the Marine Corps. During boot camp and throughout my career, I honored my vocation value by performing many jobs, developing leadership abilities, and protecting my country. After close to 10 years in the Marines, my value in holding a profession remained high. Simultaneously, I began honoring my value of learning, resumed my college education, and completed my degree. The shifts and realignment of values continued upon retirement and while opening my own business. With a focus on self-employment, my value of continuing education became a higher priority, and my value of a job shifted lower. Although I remain aware of previous values fulfilled by the Marine Corps, today I focus more attention on those aligned with business and tradecraft development. I reprioritized values I naturally outgrew so I could focus on my next important ADVENTURE. All values I have held in my past offer me the flexibility and opportunity to reprioritize them according to my desires. The amusing part about my professional life is that I satisfied my value of fun the entire time by aligning it with each experience.

Take a good look at your surroundings and activities to identify how you have shifted your values. The ones that test your ability to be RESILIENT will likely be pretty evident and easy to spot. What you unveil may offer opportunities to solve conflicts between specific values so you can reprioritize or shift them accordingly.

Changing Your Direction

To be RESILIENT does not mean we have to forge ahead. We certainly may want to reconsider other options if we jumped in too soon, didn't give enough thought, or experienced the end of a natural cycle. Although we can redesign our lives, we sometimes don't do it or don't do it well because we get stuck in our current circumstances. Instead, we continue to do what others advise or expect of us, wallow in ruts, or struggle to overcome barriers like fear. Our situations can become frustrating as we get distracted and immerse ourselves deeper. We certainly do not want to continue with what we have but are unsure whether or how to get out. So, we trudge blindly in the same direction on the same path. We will make excuses and do our best to rationalize our predicament, yet we know something has to change. Many will just suffer. Others may flat out quit and continue to look back at what was. When neither sound like good options, you have the power of RESILIENCE to look elsewhere and change direction.

Nobody wants to fail or endlessly do something they do not want to do. Knowing you have options can open possibilities to maintain the course or take a route that best suits you. But keep in mind, not all ADVENTURES are suitable for what we want in life. And as you consider all of the ways to make your ADVENTURE happen, bring with you only your old activities that will fit. You can change directions by shifting your mindset and actions based on feedback or through interpersonal relationships, tools, and technology to release those pressures. As the stress subsides, you will experience more RESILIENCE and do more of what you ENJOY in life. This concept was quite apparent with my daughter in her college years.

When she was in high school, my daughter and I made an agreement. If she received a full scholarship to any college or university, I'd gift her my little red-hot sports car. Talk about incentive! She worked hard on her grades those four years and ended up with a 4.3-grade point average. With all of the scholastic requirements met, the only thing she had left to do was wait. She applied for various schools and received quite a few acceptance letters. During her senior year, my daughter brought in the mail and opened a letter addressed to her. She was not only accepted but received confirmation of a full scholarship!

As she grew closer to leaving, she was excited and a bit nervous about VENTURING into a mostly unfamiliar degree program. After the third semester, she quickly found that she did not ENJOY Electrical Engineering (EE). During her struggles with certain classes, she sought help from professors, other students, and student teachers but still battled with grasping the major curriculum courses. She certainly didn't want to quit so she sought to switch her major. She spoke with fellow students and worked with the guidance counselor to find some answers. After a thorough examination of options, she chose the industrial systems engineering (ISE) major. She enrolled in classes at the local community college and attended summer school to catch up with the program in progress. With an answer in hand, she earned her ISE bachelor's degree and minored in business and leadership. The slight change in direction helped her be RESILIENT, take on other challenging courses, and ENJOY the rest of her time in college. Upon graduation, she grew in excitement for the new ADVENTURES that awaited her.

Quitting with Dignity

People quit all the time. Things like home projects, self-help programs, diets, budgets, and, of course, New Year's resolutions all get busted. But keep in mind that leaving things behind is natural and necessary for growth. The idea here is not that you quit or what you quit. What makes the difference is why and how. You have the freedom to stay where you are or move on. Unfortunately, both choices are often made with limited consideration or more so out of fear than desire. If you quit, you may be afraid of loss, security, criticism, or pain, yet staying the course can create the same feelings. Knowing what is truly important to you will help you push those fears aside and look at your situations more objectively. Sometimes the best answer is to move on.

We have many reasons to stop certain activities or let go of certain things. The most common and straightforward explanation is we outgrow them. We know this because we have outgrown suckling on bottles and pacifiers, using sippy cups, and wearing diapers. Other causes to move on include threats to personal security, safety, health, reputation, values, etc. Examples of these include smoking cigarettes, driving intoxicated, engaging in extreme sports, consuming certain foods, divorcing a spouse, and the list goes on.

In order to know when to quit, we set boundaries and limitations to guide us. These help us determine our red flags, gut feelings, and intuitive thoughts. Through your boundary, you draw a line that something or some event has to occur that triggers you to make a decision. Your limitation is the line you draw for yourself of what you are willing to do or accept. For example, we have better chances to increase our life expectancy when we eat healthy than when we do not. Basically, good nutrition strengthens your body, protects against diseases, and helps your digestive system. A healthier body, increases opportunities for longer life, less pain, and optimizing your bodily functions. By setting boundaries with your dietary and fitness behaviors, you determine the level of weakness, disease, and bodily dysfunctions you are willing to endure. Without boundaries, you end up blindly reacting to your health issues and limit your ability to think clearly. Times like these are when we most often get stuck and give up out of defeat. With proper planning, we can quit what we're doing with the least disruption or destruction. And by giving yourself more time to respond, you can consider more solutions on how to quit with less stress and fewer limitations. Do not wait too long, however, or the situation will grow more intense. If you decide to quit any of your set goals, bear in mind that stopping too soon may also limit growth, encourage us to quit more often, and lose faith in ourselves. Regardless, you get to decide if you are willing to commit to a new ADVENTURE or be RESILIENT and move forward in the current one.

> *Assess your limits and consider all options before you set boundaries. Set boundaries based on your values and honor them. When the time is right, you will intentionally and quickly know what to do.*

As you contemplate your thoughts of quitting and look at your choices, consider what will happen and how your decision will affect your life. Keep in mind that everything has two sides. Ideas are often considered good and bad. Emotions have happy and sad. Objects have a right and left. The list of these opposites can go on to eternity. While making your decision, if you focus heavily on either side, you will find yourself off balance. Without being centered, you will feel unsettled and pulled away from the life you deserve to ENJOY. To better ground yourself, consider the pros and cons of each choice, including doing nothing. Thoughtful considerations of all sides will help you let go of fixed judgments and determine if your values align with your proposed decision. With a calculated selection, you uphold your dignity and personal power to choose based on what is most important to you. This process will help you release the potential for regret or remorse and encourage peace with your choice to see those things fade or be part of your ADVENTURE.

Law of Threes – A third party always balances the other two through neutrality. It is where positive and negative come into balance - we become grounded, neutral, and objective.

A common example of this is when someone wants to quit a job. I've worked with many professionals transitioning from one job to another. When we begin, I always ask what they want and what's important to them. These first couple of questions drive them to identify what they value in

> *Extract the lessons from anything you quit. It is not wasted time but more a part of your journey. There's a reason for everything! It's not about reaching the end, but what you learned and how you grew in the process. If you do not learn from it, you'll repeat the same lessons until you do.*

their work. Most of the answers I receive are about a good environment, challenging work, or adequate pay. I then ask them to describe the positive and negative effects of what's going on where they are now or in their last job. Some clients were simply ready to move on. Others realized the goodness they had where they were and worked through the challenges. Although people move on for various other reasons, in my experience, only those who suffered health problems from environmental stress flat-out quit their jobs. Quite often, that may be the best solution when the trouble situations are beyond our ability to control or influence. We each set our own boundaries and the limitations we are willing to endure and go from there. No matter the circumstances, we make our own choices.

Feedback not Fail

One of the primary reasons we do or don't quit is we may see either or both as a failure. If we give up, we have failed to see it through. If we stick to it and fall short of our expectations, we have failed to get the result we sought. Failure can be devastating, but if we consider it merely feedback, we will learn to be more RESILIENT through what worked as intended and what didn't. In his book, *The Magic of thinking Big*, David Schwartz, Ph.D. states, "The difference between success and failure is found in one's

> *Share your failures with others. The lessons you learned from one person's failure may lead to another's successful learning experience. When you let others know what did not work for you, they have the opportunity to make different choices or experience their own lessons.*

attitude toward setbacks, handicaps, discouragements, and other disappointing situations." If you can shift your perspective to adopt a new attitude from that lens, you will EMBRACE failure as a feedback learning tool versus a total flop. The two feedback systems for us to consider are internal and external.

Your internal feedback system is a compilation of your encouraging or sabotaging thoughts and feelings about what you have done. In many cases, your experiences may also stimulate an external feedback system to inform you of another's perceptions of your performance or skills. Both internal and external feedback help identify areas where you flow smoothly or unwittingly sabotage your efforts. It is important to evaluate all feedback in a deliberate constructive manner so you consider areas of potential personal improvement in your behavior, thoughts, or emotions. As you become aware of your inner and outer feedback, you will soon see that there are no failures, only opportunities to consider your RESILIENCE or different ways to get things done. You must look at both from an open-minded perspective. Who knows, what you come up with may help others too.

Taming Internal Saboteurs

Self-talk is natural, whether we do so out loud or in our heads. We do it all of the time. The more challenging our endeavors are, the more vocal we become. The more extroverted we are, the more tendency we will have to think things through out loud. Conversely, people with introverted personalities process thoughts more often inside their heads. Spoken or unspoken, they are part of our internal feedback system. It tells us what we like or dislike, what's hard and easy, and whether to hang in there or quit. This inner dialogue can either help us or destroy our confidence in our efforts.

What we think or say about ourselves affects how we feel about people, things, and events in our world. In a sense, this approach can be helpful to generate ideas or, on the flip side, can cause feelings of superiority or inferiority. We touched on this challenge in EMBRACE so we can detach our comparisons of where we and others are in our journeys. We also addressed them in UPLIFT so that we see each other as equally challenged in different parts of our growth and lives. Here, we want to encourage our RESILIENCE by recognizing we all have strengths and celebrating them. Our unconscious feelings of superiority and inferiority have their upsides and downsides but generally produce positive internal results when considered with reason and without increased emotion.

From a positive perspective, superiority thoughts allow you to see your strengths and offer you confidence, self-worth, and self-value. Alternatively, they can drive you to seek external validation, ignore your mistakes, and make careless decisions. Inferiority thoughts, however, generate fears of unworthiness, uncertainty, and insecurity. Conversely, seeing others' strengths can help you pause, reflect on what you value, and research before making further decisions. Just remember, both superiority and inferiority can sabotage your RESILIENCE and drive you to quit. Balance is key to resolving inner conflict and helps you remain confident yet humble in your life.

Throughout my life, I EMBRACED the power of positive thinking and felt like I could do anything. These thoughts have offered me opportunities to experience success in various areas of my life. They have also led me to make a host of hasty decisions and mistakes along the way. Each taught me humbling lessons and uncovered opportunities for growth in each area of leadership, fitness, relationships, money, etc. Instead of dwelling on mistakes and stopping altogether, I used my lessons and, through positive thinking for prospects of success, formed incentives to take chances and resume growth. I believe life is about developing and growing; we cannot do so without risk. Yet I had to learn that not everything was for me to do. To this day, I still use the power of positive thinking, but now with a twist. I believe anything is possible if I am ready and willing to do what it takes and see it through. Each degree of effort I am willing to put into something generates feedback about what worked and what did not. Not everything requires the same effort, and I am not on this planet to accomplish everything. I excel in certain areas, but someone will always be better, faster, and stronger than me. Accepting that belief as a natural order of things has brought me peace. I get to choose the most empowering yet humbling ADVENTURES that help me grow, little by little. You can do the same through a balanced consideration of self-feedback.

Law of Self-destruction - You will destroy yourself with too much or not enough challenge. That which is totally successful destroys itself. Unless you challenge yourself, you will stand still and stagnate. Work toward balance through wise risk.

Managing External Saboteurs

External influences can also pose a significant effect on our ability to be RESILIENT. As life goes on, the things, people, and events we experience will propel us forward, slow us down, or stop us. These occurrences offer clues as to whether our outer world produced our inner desires. When our external world is not supportive, it steals our time, crowds our space, and drains our energy. Unless managed, the resulting impact taxes our ability to be open-minded, patient, and proactive.

Feedback can often be hard to accept when all we see and hear is that we have failed. We receive feedback from everywhere and everybody. We've been graded our entire lives through schooling, parental guidance, work evaluations, and simply existing. Every opinion about us or of how we perform is based on an external standard that is frequently different from facts or our own reality. Recognizing that feedback is oftentimes subjective allows you to let go of doubt, fear, and concern about another's thoughts, words, and actions. Consider the feedback only to test what you know and what you choose to accept from others. Research what you do not know, and use your mind to generate your own outcome. Only you can choose what you want to believe. When you reach this point, it's up to you to stop seeking external validation and begin living in peace with the world around you.

#46 euclid – be curious beyond what you know currently as fact. Although still true today, we have greatly advanced geometry beyond the foundation of these two axioms, "a point is that which has no part" and "a line is a length without breadth." Humans have so much more to learn!

Thomas Edison said it well in his famous phrase about the lightbulb, "I have not failed 10,000 times—I've successfully found 10,000 ways that will not work." He did not allow external feedback to sabotage his efforts but diligently tested what he observed, heard, and learned from others to create the lightbulb we use today. Do your best to be open and test different ideas, so you can clear known obstacles, determine what is ideal for you, and stay RESILIENT through other challenges that may appear.

Law of Self-truth – Truth works for you and you only. Be careful of what you accept as your truth. It will influence all aspects of your life and your future.

Clear Obstacles

One of the biggest obstacles in our ability to be RESILIENT is negativity. Very few people ENJOY negativity, yet they refuse to remove the problems that cause it. Most often, it's because they struggle to fully recognize what actually adds value to their journey. Indeed, if we have yet to identify the value in our goal, but still know it is important, one of the most effective ways to be RESILIENT is to clear those barriers that stand in our way. When you removing these obstacles, you quickly see what needs to happen and what tools or abilities you have or may need for your ADVENTURE. Carefully consider what to keep around, save for later, or remove as certain things may come in handy later.

One of the biggest problems in clearing obstacles is facing them, especially when they are people. It's one thing to throw away stuff and stop wasting your time, but it's another to approach people for help or space. Sometimes the value they bring is not understood, especially when we perceive it as unfavorable. We do not want to surround ourselves with people who tell us we are doing something wrong, but their input may be valuable and something you should hear. Nevertheless, as stated above, we need to know our boundaries and limitations and communicate our concerns in a kind manner. As a good friend and International Best-Selling Author, Elizabeth Duncan-Hawker wrote in her book, *Collecting True Friends*, "Choose your words wisely because they carry real power. One word can UPLIFT a soul or crush it." If you think about it, many people are trying to help. Just like us, sometimes their help does not help at all, yet they will not know if you do not tell them.

> ✒ *Be open, kind, and honest with important the people in your life. Most want to be involved and see you succeed. Through sincere conversations, you save precious relationships!*

Sometimes we, unfortunately, need to endure the pain of parting with particular people, activities, and things along our journey. These relationships are usually the unhealthy ones that conflict with your values. Holding onto painful attachments strips away your ability to learn and ENJOY. Yet ridding yourself of them can trigger guilt, shame, fear, and a relentless neediness. For instance, if you remain in toxic, draining, and uncooperative relationships, you may build barriers that stop you from pursuing your goals. Once again, you will know when to say goodbye by honoring your boundaries and knowing your limitations. Perhaps you are on the path to a healthier diet. You'll want to clear your cabinets and refrigerator of self-sabotaging food items. By keeping these foods out of immediate reach, you will have to make an effort to get them. Another example is if you want to advance your education. You will need to clear your calendar of certain events so you can schedule in your courses. Honor your values and move beyond your unhelpful emotions tied to your attachments. Eventually, you will alter your external environment to support your inner desires with the least disruption.

> *Pay attention to what's standing in your way. Either EMBRACE it as it is or let it go. The power is in your hands to clear your path from obstructions. When you do, be kind and send them off with love and appreciation for the lessons they leave behind.*

Visualize Success Along the Way

To ensure we are on the right track, we would be well served to pause and rest our minds and bodies every once in a while. We may not have thoroughly considered the details of our initial idea. By becoming present and paying attention to what is going on, you will increase your RESILIENCE. Take a little time to EMBRACE where you are in your ADVENTURE, assess what's been going on, and reimagine the outcome with more specific details. You may have had to be flexible and take unexpected paths for various reasons. Although sometimes necessary, where you seem to have landed may have muddled the vision of your intended course. What once was clear may now look quite distorted or be more distant than expected. If you do not get back on track with what is most

> *Reimagine what you want continuously. Application is more powerful than knowledge. Imagination is more powerful than application. Without imagination, application will never happen.*

significant, you may falter in fulfilling your ADVENTURE. As you reimagine the steps, you can better monitor your progress and ensure proper alignment. This activity can take little to no effort, but it may demand much practice and faith in yourself.

Sometimes we can also get so hyper-focused on doing and achieving milestones that we do not recognize when we would have been better off modifying our approach. Neither staying the course nor going a different route is right or wrong. Beautiful things can happen either way. A pause allows you to clear your thoughts and contemplate if your direction aligns with your desires and benefits you. When your mind clears of couldas and shouldas, you open space to visualize what you want next. Also, if any thoughts come up telling you that you should be doing something else, pay attention enough to write it down and let it go to consider later. Concentrate on each completed step, including whoever is involved. Embody it through sight, sound, touch, smell, and taste. Basically, live each experience as if you have it right then and there. While you are at it, use your intuition to guide you to your answers. It is your body's internal feedback watchdog that informs you if something seems suitable or misdirected. Listen for the answers from inside you. I do this quite often and sometimes receive some amazing feedback.

When I began my writing ADVENTURE, I worked with my business coach, Cynthia, to determine what I wanted to create and extract ideas for the chapters. I had a lot of energy going into notebooks, journals, flipcharts, and so much more. After six months, I started to feel stressed but wrote it off as anxieties about writing my first book. The pressure went on for days, and I continued to push. One morning I decided to forego my regular meditation routine and did something a little different: a body check. Everything felt okay until I reached the top of my left shoulder. I felt a dull pain, like a thumb pressed down hard into it. As I paused and contemplated what that was, I realized I was stressed about my book. I was confused. The book was my choice, and nobody pressured me to do it or held me to a timeframe. Apparently, how I was approaching the complex and complicated material was putting a lot of pressure on me. I trusted that I would eventually receive an answer to move forward. During breakfast, I noticed a saying on my coffee mug, "Life is my favorite ADVENTURE." This thoughtful gift from my coach was precisely the message I sought to push aside my approach to the old book. With a commitment to myself to publish a book, I experienced internal images and messages to help me decide on the content you are reading today. As I expected, I have not felt that pain in my shoulder ever since.

Pay attention to signs from your body and surroundings and question their validity as to whether you should stay the course or depart it. It could be a feeling of excitement that will keep you sharp, stretch your abilities, and catapult some personal or professional growth. The more challenging it is, the more you will grow, feel accomplished, and possibly want to do it again. We simply need to pause, visualize, and pay attention to what your internal feedback mechanisms tell you.

Resource or Resign

A new VENTURE usually energizes people. Yet sometimes, even when our vision is clear and we overcome stumbling blocks, we may still struggle to stay the course. We might just need help and are not sure where or how to get it. Oftentimes, when we do not deal with it quickly, we give up. Through our resourcefulness, we can gather the tools and people to help keep us on track and pull through.

Resourcing can be a very challenging hurdle in our lives. Resource scarcity is one main reason most people resign from jobs, falter in relationships, and quit businesses. They are missing something that they either expected to be there when they started or were not sure how to get for themselves. They hit a wall, get stuck, and become frustrated. Eventually, joy slips away or the ADVENTURE begins to feel like hard labor. Yet, many people do not consider that an unrecognized need for resources might be the true problem.

Resource shortages can cascade from a lack of knowledge, tools, and people to help you. If you do not have the knowledge, you will struggle to know who or what can help. Tools require knowledge and skills that, if lacking, you will need to rely on others to help you through. People are one of our biggest resources as they often come with the tools and knowledge to use them. When you learn how to use resources wisely, you will conquer the struggles of performing previously complex, laborious, or tedious work. If you do not know who or what is available, you may end up throwing in the towel. Before you resign from your goals, discover what you need and ask for help. You will then have the ability to harness the power of your resources and keep moving forward.

> *Use your resources or surrender to mediocrity. Problems are hard enough to solve. Before you submit to failure or quit, surround yourself with the best knowledge, tools, technology, and people.*

Law of Abundance - We live in a world of endless resources. EMBRACE what you have right now and be wise when choosing who and what you bring into your world.

Knowledge Upgrades

One of the best parts of achieving anything is what you learn along the way. But what is most meaningful is when you realize about who you have become in the process. Your new abilities and skills can be applied over and over again. Just remember, the amount of your current knowledge is limited, but EMBRACE continuous learning since the potential for self-development is limitless and builds RESILIENCE.

> ⚡ *Adopt continuous learning as a means to RESILIENCE. Successful completion is not about what you know at the end. It's about self-discovery and sparking a drive to continue learning.*

Many of us go through life thinking we have to know everything. We want to be the go-to person for everyone. It makes us feel needed, influential, and intelligent and feeds our desire for self-actualization. There is nothing wrong with these grand appeals until we allow them to overpower our desire for continued growth. Our growth slows when we shut ourselves off from other perspectives and pressure others to agree with us. People often defend their need to be right because it is true for them. They may also reject other perspectives or omit facts because they do not want to be embarrassed or feel stupid, ignorant, or foolish. People often use these tactics to dominate or get attention from others. These behaviors can ruin relationships, sabotage goals, and block our ability to learn. Consider this: facts are gathered by effort. The truth reveals itself effortlessly.

#42 moment of truth – the moment we stand up to what we believe is true and find it's not can be a grim reality for us. Question your own intentions before you question others.

Accept the truth that you will never know everything, nor must you. Of the 2.4 million terabytes of information, we categorize, delete, and distort, most people forget 50%

in the first hour of learning and 75% within 24 hours. That number gets even larger if we do not constantly review or use the material. For example, if you speak a foreign language and stop for a long time, you will likely forget many of its nuances until you practice again.

You have a baseline knowledge derived from your many past interests and experiences. As you become curious and expand your horizons, the desire for more information will naturally grow. Be curious like a child. Open your mind to learn more and seize opportunities. Even experts continue learning, testing, and comparing their discoveries with past experiences and colleagues. Recognize that you are already bright and allow others' lights to shine. Admit when you do not know something and agree to learn more often. Allow people to finish their sentences without trying to read their minds. You never know what golden nuggets you will soon discover. The bright nuggets can help us realize that we still have so much more to learn.

> *Be fascinated by what you learn instead of fascinating others with what you know. People who know more and want to become more intelligent listen more and speak less.*

Law of Knowledge - Knowledge is power but only if used. It becomes valuable when you use it for the good of self and all.

Cool Tools and Technology

Our tools and technology can make the most daunting, tedious tasks seem to disappear. But, if we do not learn to use tools and technology wisely, they will soon and unkindly take control over us. We see this daily with televisions, cell phones, computers, gaming devices, etc. Tools and technology are very powerful assets that can keep us going strong, but, in the same breath, they can also weaken us.

Tools and technology are often labeled the same thing and used similarly in terms of resourcing. The difference is that tools are what we use, and technologies are what enhance them. Technology makes our tools faster, stronger, easier, and more effective. A simple tool appropriate for a job can enhance your confidence that projects will come together the way you want. If you become frustrated with your tools, it's very likely that they may be unsuitable for the job or are old, worn out, or broken to some degree. Reduce your frustration by ditching and possibly replacing them.

If you desire new tools, buy, rent, or borrow them and learn how to use them. If time is of the essence, find someone who already knows how to use them and learn from them or hire them. In the end, you will feel more capable and generate pride in the outcome. There is nothing like using cool tools to get the job done! They make work so much easier, quicker, and more precise.

We often experience complications with our tools when we include technology in the equation. Technology increases our tool capability in so many ways, such as saving time, making information accessible, enhancing learning capabilities, propelling innovation, and many other benefits. We see this in action in transportation, agriculture, medicine, banking, construction, energy, and manufacturing, among other markets. Technology has vastly improved our abilities to connect with people, create products with more accuracy and efficiency, learn independently, and strengthen our feelings of security. Our challenges with technology lie in the learning curve associated with implementing them. They can be too cumbersome and frustrating to learn. They might be less challenging if you think of them as another opportunity to learn and grow. If time is on your side or you can schedule it into your calendar, test the bells and whistles and have fun with them. Through patience and play, you can hone your RESILIENCE and ENJOY.

Frustration is not the only aspect of technology that disrupts our goals. They can become even more troublesome when we are unable to put them down or do without them. They train us to rely on them in many areas of both our personal and professional lives. Sometimes we become so addicted to technology that it inhibits our growth and abilities. It slows our activity levels, decreases meaningful connections with people, encourages procrastination, and reduces our memory, plus many other negative effects. We can end up losing sleep, wrecking relationships, creating anxiety and depression, and even hindering our ability to learn. To use technology effectively, bring a balanced approach and as much self-control as you can muster.

> ✒ *Balance your technology use. Use them intentionally for productive purposes. When finished, turn them off and put them away.*

Some people say that technology makes us dumber. Others say it allows us to become more creative and innovative. Like everything, it is all in how we use it and balance it in our lives. Let's face it. Technology is a vital part of our world and here to stay. The point of using technology is to make sure that it serves to enhance our lives, not let it run them. When we take our power back from technology, we are often surprised to discover how much time and attention we relinquished to it. With a more deliberate approach to technology, we will regain our focus and apply it toward finishing what we started or move on to a new VENTURE.

> **Law of Limitless - We live in a world of endless possibility and resources.**

My Peeps

People can be one of your greatest resources to help keep you on track. When you tap into your people resources, you stay connected through information exchange, expanded learning, and positive impressions. They can help you pull ideas and thoughts you already knew even before becoming stuck. They also teach you fresh things you did not know existed. They can support and encourage you to keep moving forward and do more than you ever thought possible. Most of all, people genuinely want to see you succeed. When you reach out to other people for their help, you also offer them an opportunity to shine their light. This makes them feel competent, valued, and trusted. It also shows that you appreciate their uniqueness, talents, and expertise.

Expert Service

Let's be honest with ourselves. Some tasks we simply should not waste our time doing. We can easily recognize situations and seek help where we lack expertise, talent, or complex knowledge. The ones we grapple with most are the other activities we know how to do, are physically capable of doing, but do not want to do. In our attempt to be frugal, we say we are going to do them ourselves. Instead, we continuously procrastinate until they become too much to handle all at once. They soon clutter our minds, create chaos, consume our time, and drain our energy. Although we want to be RESILIENT and overcome our stalling, we end up self-defeated.

The effects of procrastination can drag us down and pull us away from what we want to accomplish. As soon as we identify these activities, we know it's time to employ some help. Whether we pay, barter, or borrow, we have plenty of options to attain and use expert services. For instance, every year, we pay the local nursery to deliver ten yards of mulch for our garden beds and under the trees. They stage it where we want, and I spread it throughout the yard. If our schedules do not permit, we hire their staff to complete the entire job. We have the option to do all of it ourselves, but the nursery is more equipped and efficient in delivering than we are in picking it up. By relying on this expert service, I am able to concentrate time on reaching my three goals of exercise, beautification, and plant care with the same task.

You can tap into all types of professional resources, such as architects, landscapers, engineers, tutors, lawyers, organizers, house cleaners, doctors, and the list goes on forever. You also do not have to settle for one person. The market is filled with different experience levels, price points, and styles. Once again, you have the power to choose who you want to work for you. It is also your choice how to free up your time to focus on what is most important to you!

Expert Advice

One of the most compelling reasons to have any ADVENTURE is the thrill of the entire experience. We often do not want others to become too involved in the process, as they may take away our opportunity to master ambitious tasks that offer the most growth. When the challenges become too tricky, and we experience little to no success in our attempt to find answers, it may be time to seek expert advice. With expert advice, we can collect different knowledge points and choose what will best help us see our goal through to completion.

Oddly enough, even after great lengths of time spent looking for help, people still often find it hard to ask for advice. And when they do, they do not always follow it. Sometimes we simply do not know who to trust. We've all heard about mechanics who will try to sell us a whole new engine when all we wanted was an oil change. You may also have been offered conflicting advice from two experts and did not know which to choose. It is often a good practice to get other viewpoints from people, especially in significant areas of your life, such as health and finances. But sometimes we have so many options that we find it hard to know which one to choose. Seriously, look at all of the diet and exercise programs out there. Maybe we would have an easier time choosing one if they explained the benefits of each in a manner we could understand. Although these things sometimes happen, we shouldn't let instances like these stop us from seeking advice. The reality is that asking for advice is a personal pursuit and a sign of intelligence. The point is not to accept everything you hear. Carefully consider aspects of the information provided and intentionally come to your own conclusions on how to apply it. Sometimes the outcome will be great. If it isn't, do your best to be flexible and choose other options until you find one that works. Even secondhand advice can be invaluable and help us be RESILIENT.

Jimmy, a close friend, was in that situation when he decided to run his first marathon at age 50. Jimmy had always thought about running 26.2 miles, was unsure how to do it, and wanted advice. He asked if I would help him train, and I excitedly agreed. Although I had run a few marathons and knew a bit about completing them, I was still a bit of a rookie. But Jimmy already had a baseline of running, so, just like I did for my first marathon, I offered him suggestions based on his current knowledge and skills. Jimmy did as I suggested and started his marathon VENTURE. Because his goal was to finish it in a respectable time and uninjured, I gave Jimmy some sage training advice I had received during my first race.

On race day, I offered Jimmy another piece of advice that I neglected to take during my first marathon. To help him avoid the 'bonk' that marathon runners experience when they feel the exhilarating start rush, he was to run at a slower pace out of the starting line than he wanted. Jimmy paced himself well until about 22 to 23 miles when I saw him walking. With some fun bantering between us, I encouraged him to start running again and told him not to let me beat him to the finish line. Jimmy surged through the finish line as tears of pride welled up inside of him. He knew he finished strong and could not believe he had completed 26.2 miles in the time he did. Because Jimmy took the advice and used what worked for him during training and the race, his RESILIENCE carried him through one of the toughest endurance runs. I was super proud of Jimmy and myself as both of us achieved new personal records. Sometimes it's not only the advice but the partnerships that can help pull you both through.

> *Choose wisely the advice you receive. Identify how it fits into your future. Carefully choosing can help you let go of memories of failure from your past, turn them into present wisdom, and use them for future experiences.*

There is no shortchange of expert advice. We can get it from many sources, like consultants, mentors, specialists, advisors, etc. Just like you are an expert in your work and life, everyone has their own expertise that differs from yours. Pros are very skilled in their particular job and clearly understand what works for them. They can advise you in professional areas of health, careers, money, parenting, medicine, and more. They can also help you manage your personal world with organization skills, time management, and relationship-building, to name a few. Since we all know there is more than one way to get things done, these advisors will offer their perspectives and lessons learned in their own experiences. As an added benefit, asking for advice goes beyond a mere information exchange. It also creates trusted, honest, closer relationships and friendships. If you decided to VENTURE into something new and got stuck, expert advice would likely offer ideas in fields of study that you may never have imagined.

Expert Partnerships

When we are stuck or feel like we lag behind, we may need someone to help us reveal what is keeping us there and create solutions to get beyond it. Partners can do just that. They offer moral support, encouragement, more opportunities, and different perspectives. Like consultants and mentors, they bring their own expertise and work with your goals in mind. The difference is partners do not steer you with their knowledge as much as they encourage you and draw out your greatness. Basically, like coaches, they do not tell you what to do but help light a fire in you to promote movement toward what you want in a manner appropriate for you.

Partners can come in many forms. On the business side, you can have active, dormant, nominal, etc. Some of these professionals agree to build and sustain a business throughout its lifetime. Other business coaches and consultants can guide you through your business's creative and managerial process and possibly areas of life affected by your work. On the personal side, expert partnerships include romantic, exercise, spiritual, intellectual, creative, and anyone who guides you on your journey. Since they help you develop your skills,

Describe in detail what you want in any type of partner. Be honest with yourself about the degree you are willing to contribute to the partnership. Each of you has a role and must be enabled to fulfill it completely.

overcome hurdles, and help you grow, you will want someone honest, direct, kind, sensible, resourceful, consistent, and compatible with your energy. Chemistry and mutual respect are keys to finding an expert partner who will help you build the courage to face challenges head-on.

Law of Association - Two or more shared interests that generate energy through similarity, pleasure or pain, repetition, and attention can influence an outcome.

Expert Champions

We all can benefit from surrounding ourselves with people who cheer for our success! These enthusiastic people encourage, motivate, and energize us. They help you feel good about yourself, shift your attitude, attract more friends, and keep focused while encouraging you to accomplish your goals. When you hear their positive words, you will feel more committed and get more done. You will see changes in yourself with less stress and more drive. By surrounding yourself with positive influences, you will reduce your stress level, improve your performance, and feel more control over your life.

We see variations of positive and negative energy quite often in work environments. The funny thing is, it only takes one person to shift that energy. Most of us know what it was like to work in our favorite job and for an exceptional boss. We felt encouraged, empowered, and inspired to do our best. Marcus Buckingham hit the nail on the head when he said, "People leave managers, not companies." When faced with persistent negativity, we become reluctant to try harder, innovate, or speak up. The ripple effect can be vast and lasting if not met with positivity, inspiration, and respect. Although undesirable feedback will still occur, how you handle it makes all the difference. Expert champions deliver the best in their ability to help you be optimistic, proactive, and inspired to stay the course.

As you consider who will offer you the best encouragement, assess your self-control, satisfaction, and approach to life. Then, determine if you are focused on a positive directions or falling into a negative energy trap. Next, think about the people in your life and notice who tends to hold a positive attitude. If they consistently encourage you and offer constructive feedback in a candid but hopeful manner, keep them around. For people who tend to be negative and have difficulty trusting their own actions, invite their input sparingly. Be open, but only to words that can help you live your life fully.

Sometimes, even just one person is all it takes to encourage you to put your best foot forward. In our family, my champion has been my sister Erika. Whenever I needed reassurance or an UPLIFT, Erika was there to help. From childhood through many major life events, she encouraged me to do my best, offered sage feedback, and stood beside me the whole way. Erika consoled me, celebrated with me, visited me at duty stations, and participated in life-changing events, such as my military retirement, marathons, and cross-country coaching events. She would cheer for me and all who participated. Erika was notably one of my biggest champions during my most significant transitions into executive and leadership coaching. She volunteered to participate in certification training processes, wisdom hikes, and my first-ever retreat. Erika's encouragement and support continued as we VENTURED to different parts of the world together. We shared inspiring experiences in Peru, South Korea, and various destinations along the US east coast, north, and deep south. Erika has been the most positive, encouraging champion throughout my life. I am forever grateful to her for enriching my life with her positivity, inspiration, and support during times of celebration and difficulty.

> ⚡ *Pay attention to the effect positivity has on you. If you are not encouraged, motivated, or committed, you may need to face your negative emotions. Do not dismiss them as they are valid! EMBRACE them all, give THANKS for what they reveal, and harness the positive while letting the negative flow through you.*

The more champions you invite into your life, the more energy you will generate to enhance your RESILIENCE. This shared enthusiasm taps into your pride to help you stand tall and be confident. It doesn't stop there! Your champions, along with all of your other resources, will also help keep you in a state of flow with your endeavors, so you feel less forced. The positive energy you generate will be inclined to UPLIFT others through a boost in your morale.

Flow or Force

As we covered in VENTURE, we should begin any activity intentionally and with willpower. If it's something we did not want to do from the start, we would feel forced to continue, which may lead us to procrastinate. The same can be said for roles only we can perform to achieve our bigger goals. Perhaps you do not ENJOY doing taxes, yet you know they must be completed to receive a return from an overpayment or spare yourself a hefty fine or jail time. To process them, you may force yourself to do the work or hire somebody else. Either way, they cannot be completed until you gather all of the relative information. Sometimes, these tedious chores can be draining. For situations like this, you must choose to face it head on and push yourself into action. By using your willpower, you stretch your growth to finish what you started and enhance your RESILIENCE skills.

Most of the time, we will drive ourselves to meet basic human needs of stability, variety, belonging, worth, etc. The water can become muddy when we extend beyond these fundamental needs to identify what we want next. It's harder to discern what moves to make, if any, especially if we yearn for something that conflicts with our beliefs about our needs and values. You may find yourself avoiding certain activities or excessively pushing to get what you want. This resistance or overpowering force tends to repel instead of attract what you want in your life. Check your actions to determine if you are forcing your will or allowing it to help you naturally unfold your experience. This natural unfolding is where flow comes into play. Some people say that you are in your Zone when you are in flow. Ultimately, in your *Zone of Potential*, flow is a way to recognize when you are performing optimally along your path toward your purest potential.

Flow is a state of being where you feel as if you and your ADVENTURE are the only things that exist at that moment. When you are in flow, you are willing to do whatever it takes to accomplish your goal. It is a high state of love for your activity where everything seems to stand still even as you move along. You are so entirely absorbed that everything around you seems not to exist. The outcome is not forced but flows, like a DANCER, composer, motorcycle rider, athlete, etc. Mihaly Csikszentmihalyi, in his book, *Flow: The Psychology of Optimal Experience*, explains flow as "the state in which people are so involved in an activity that nothing else seems to matter; the experience itself is so ENJOYABLE that people do it even at great costs, for the sheer sake of doing it." When you are in flow, you feel completely alive, remarkably flexible, and a calm excitement no matter what happens. Flow comes when you clearly know what you want, and activities join together to make the process faster and easier. By joining intention, willpower, and finesse of your DANCE, you do not go with the flow as much as you flow with the go. With flow, you reinforce your ability to be RESILIENT and create a sense of ease through difficult situations.

People who participate in extreme or intense sports experience flow state quite often. When Johnny raced motorcycles, he would sometimes go over 175 miles per hour, drag his knees and elbows on the concrete, and respond to the bike's moves in split seconds. During his best performances, Johnny rode so fast and smoothly that everything slowed down and time seemed to stand still for him. Any shift in focus or loss of confidence in himself or the bike would alter Johnny's perception of time during the race and affect his performance. Everything seemed to move and happen so simply and quickly that his reaction time became compressed. He said racing was like ballet on two wheels where, together, he and his bike were one synergistic power defying time. They were undoubtedly in a flow state together. Although you may not have participated in these types of sports, you may very well have encountered these same experiences during other activities in your life.

Law of Dominant Desire - A stronger emotion will dominate the weaker one and influence everything you do and everything you are.

Crystal Clear Purpose

Sometimes, we can become so entrenched in our activities that we forget why we were heading down particular paths from the start. This observation can become evident when we hit a crossroads and are uncertain about what to do next. The depth of our involvement may be so intense that we neglect the purpose of our actions and slip back into meeting immediate unfulfilled needs instead. Because the activities are very familiar, we tend to fall easily into our comfort zone and coast along. Sooner or later, we may find ourselves lost without a compass and unsatisfied. We may want to give up altogether. If you hit this juncture, it is definitely an excellent time to reacquaint yourself with your purpose and maybe even tweak your attitude. In fact, you do not have to wait until you hit a crossroads. To avoid getting stuck in uncertainty and stay RESILIENT, constantly review the value of what you are doing and make minor adjustments in your day to align with your purpose. Remember, your purpose is why you get up in the morning.

We have addressed purpose, or dharma, in AWAKEN and a few other times throughout the book. Your dharma is your gift or specific aim in life supported by experiences and learning. It is the fingerprint you want to make on the world. By reminding yourself of the legacy you want to leave, your attitude about what to do next can quickly shift to a more positive one. When you frequently revisit your purpose, you will soon see how your vision, mission, and actions guide you toward it.

> ⚡ *Change the way you look at things, and your entire view will seem to change. As you engage in growth opportunities, you will begin to notice activities that align with your ultimate purpose.*

All your activities tie together and create your current mission supporting your vision. With an unclear mission, you will probably feel unfocused and become distracted by your thoughts and surroundings. Although your feelings are valid, you may not have considered that your purpose was not as crystal clear when you started. Constantly clarifying your purpose may alter your current vision slightly, and ongoing activities can reveal details of what might work for your mission. At this point, you get to decide what is in your power to change, what is beyond your capability to change, and what you are willing to do next. When clarifying your purpose, the main keys to your RESILIENCE are to focus on the impact you want to produce in the world and the changes you can make within your locus of control.

For my life purpose, I feel I am here to inspire people to do, be, and have what they never thought possible. My vision is to see people at peace with themselves regardless of their situations. With my purpose and vision, I created my current

> ⚡ *Be clear on the impact you want to leave on the world. With clarity comes a true sense of purpose and mission.*

mission. I am guiding people through my sense of ADVENTURE to design their lives so they may experience more peace, joy, love, and happiness in their lives. Presently, I carry out my mission by creating this book, workshops, speaking engagements, one-on-one coaching, and various other prospects. Being clear on my purpose opens doors to many possibilities and helps me quickly identify options to fulfill my vision and mission. This continuously renewed clarity helps me stay in flow consistently. By including purposeful challenges, I stretch myself by tackling them head-on with patience, self-love, and kindness. Every change that comes with them supports my growth and strengthens my RESILIENCE. For this, I am grateful!

Synergistic Effects

As your purpose, vision, and mission become more evident, you may begin to realize why some people, activities, etc. stay with you while others drop off. That which fades away probably did not add value to your life because at least one of you did not invest the necessary attention to keep it around. Whatever persists is there because you either have yet to learn from it, or you have integrated it into your life. To maintain your flow state, you will want to know which is there for learning and which offers you the ability to be adaptable, optimistic, and open-minded.

> ⚡ *Pay attention to who and what you think about the most. Take care to not obsess with these, or you will strangle them, push them away, or lose yourself in them. For a synergistic effect, what we value must flow freely.*

Synergy is a natural flow of valuable people, items, and events that are already effective and rewarding. Although we may consider daily routines as something synergistic, do not confuse them. Our days can be thrown completely off when our routines are disrupted. Just because we use daily routines for efficient practices does not mean they are always practical. Sometimes they can tax our ability to be adaptable and RESILIENT. In order to develop flexibility and strengthen your optimism, shake up your routines a little every now and then. Not only will you improve your ability to adjust, but modifications will help you test the flexibility of your outer world. You will soon notice what is in synergy and, therefore, most important to keep in your life.

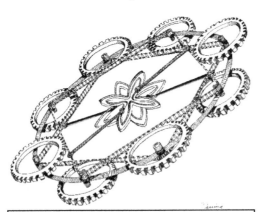

#9 ur-flower – as the center point of your life, you have many gears that connect together and create movement. Adequate eustress (good stress), strength, and smoothness will maintain the integrity of a fulfilling life!

The beauty about those synergistic aspects, people, things, and events, is that they fit easily into your life, and you consistently know how to incorporate them into every part of your world. You fit together like puzzle pieces, enhance each other, and increase collective value while co-creating a rich, vibrant picture. We can all imagine those qualities in an optimal intimate relationship, and you can also get them from other things in your life, such as work, recreation, friendships, and so on. By identifying and strengthening your synergistic powerhouse, you can generate more confidence in your ability to be RESILIENT when challenges arise and work more smoothly through them. You will find that time goes by fast and yet seems to stand still. That is when you know you are in flow!

Time Warp

To stay steadily RESILIENT and in flow, we must recognize that all things will appear and happen when we are ready for them. It is strange how time can sometimes feel like it is flying past or dragging behind us. In truth, we all know that time does not really change in pace. It is all about what we are doing at the moment that generates a disjointed sense of time. For instance, time seems to drag when we are bored, anticipate an event, or not ENJOYING something. On the other hand, time seems like it speeds up when we are excited.

Sometimes we can confuse flow with mastery. Yet, as we move about our day, we tend to pay less attention to things we have already mastered. These activities don't necessarily represent a flow state, nor do they require much RESILIENCE. We often are not present and force our external world to comply with our desires and at our own pace. This attitude can have us feeling like we are not getting anywhere and sometimes question our mastery. We want things to speed up and happen or reveal themselves in a predesignated timeframe. When they do not, we become anxious, frustrated, and maybe even a bit disoriented. After we finally experience

> *Slow down to go fast. Calming your excitement will help you focus on the details of what you are doing. You will create more efficiencies, reduce mistakes, and experience a steady speed that surpasses your expectations.*

what we want, the timeframe may have felt like an eternity. If it takes too long, we may even throw in the towel. In reality, everything happens in its own time. We will forfeit our ability to be RESILIENT if we try to force time to warp to our demands. As we open ourselves to the notion that everything has a cycle and happens when it should, we will develop our ability to be patient and flexible and allow things to occur naturally. It does not imply that we simply do absolutely nothing and wait. Instead, we can prepare for its arrival, physically, mentally, and emotionally and allow time to warp on its own.

One way to develop our patience and flexibility and virtually defy time is by trying something new. With novel experiences, we tend to slow down, expose ourselves to new ideas, and learn more about ourselves. As you focus on the latest activity, absorb relevant details, and use what you know, your energy will increase, as will your momentum. As you become more familiar and skilled in these activities, you naturally generate excitement while feeling as if time is standing still. You will be more relaxed and confident and eventually slip into the state of flow. One key consideration

> *Cherish your moments in each experience while time feels like it's moving slow. The closer you get to finishing your activities, the more time will seem to accelerate.*

for experiencing flow is, that you must be honest with yourself about your level of commitment and willingness in your new activity to create a sense of harmony with it. Otherwise, you might again get irritated and thwart your ability to feel the simplicity that flow can bring.

Simplify

We naturally gravitate toward a path of least resistance. As multi-faceted and challenging as our lives can get, it's no wonder we look for easier ways to do things. We want our lives to be smooth and uncomplicated, yet we so often overextend ourselves. Sometimes we will even overthink our activities and get stuck in the details, holding onto perfection. With all of the complexity going on, we find it harder to simplify our lives and make space for what is truly important to us. But do not fret. The trick is to align your energy toward what you value most and less on things that are not urgent. As you identify what is truly important and pressing in your life, you will create a more optimistic outlook through the simplicity you create to get things done. When you simplify your time and efforts, you will find it easier to press through the challenging distractions and disruptions because the completion will seem nearer.

You may not have ever considered the volume of distractions, excessive busyness, and mind games you currently have that can complicate your world. Consciously decide to remove these, and you will quickly and easily begin to feel the simplicity that flow has to offer. You empower yourself to stay in the groove by consistently eliminating unimportant and unurgent activities. Lack of practice will revert you back to your old habits. Indecision will keep you trapped in the stressful doubts of should, could, and would that hold you back. Instead, intentionally choose your path and repeat your success within it. You will be amazed at how RESILIENT you become, especially when other pressing matters arise.

> ⚡ *Be the decision-maker of your life. By owning and using your power of choice, you will feel more in control, tend to EMBRACE the results, and find greater RESILIENT power in your life.*

Another trick is to learn the power of a shrug. A shrug doesn't mean you do not care, but more so that you recognize events will unfold the way they will. With the world on his shoulders, Atlas knew the power of a shrug. Like Atlas, challenge yourself through high goals, but not high expectations. Do the best you can with what you have and detach yourself from achieving perfection, meeting others' expectations, and succumbing to others' demands. Adopt a neutral mindset to take pressure off of yourself and accept things for what they are. With this outlook, you can overcome challenges with greater flexibility, patience, and balance. It can also help you build RESILIENCE in the face of rejection when you are told no or want to say no. Do your best to keep in the back of your mind that an ENJOYABLE life requires simplicity. By combining the

> ⚡ *Release expectations of the outcome. You sacrifice the ease and simplicity of your creation when you force your agenda. As you let go of expectations, you allow opportunities to flow to you. There is a reason for*

vital aspects of focus, synergy, timing, and simplicity, you significantly strengthen your RESILIENCE to overcome incredible odds. Ultimately, when you are in flow, you will not feel like you need to be RESILIENT. You will recognize that you already are.

Law of Circulation – What comes from you goes around and comes back to you.

Chapter 10

ENJOY

*E*very one of us are on the journey of life to discover our meaning. As you AWAKEN to how you have created your life, you'll begin to recognize and maybe even appreciate the many experiences you have encountered. Our primary purpose as creators is in the service to ourselves and others. And similar to our purpose, happiness, love, joy, and peace are all related to these ideals and deeply rooted at our core. This is not to imply that you ENJOYED all of your circumstances, but you can be proud of what you've accomplished and the impact your contributions left on others. To ENJOY life, harness your talents, use your life lessons, and create something miraculous. When you EMBRACE your successes, you open the doors to discover a more profound meaning and greater happiness in life.

> *Harmonize your emotions. Offset negative emotions, i.e., sadness, fear, lack, anger, etc. with love, compassion, forgiveness, and THANKS. You will find that you are more willing and accepting and see things in a balanced view. From this perspective, you'll experience and offer others love, joy, and peace.*

ENJOY Happiness Within

Many of us in the world today are in continuous pursuit of happiness. Even though we experience the full spectrum of emotions, people can choose and practice happiness. It helps us cope with life challenges, increases productivity, and improves our interpersonal relationships. The high energy that happiness generates can improve your health, deepen relationships, and offer greater feelings of THANKFULNESS. It's no wonder that people are in constant pursuit of it. The problem is when we blindly push to be perpetually happy and ignore less than pleasing aspects. We disregard unpleasant feelings and allow them to fester inside. We may become numb to misfortunes with ourselves and others. We also shortchange the opportunity to EMBRACE challenges, use them to kick us into action, and turn them into positive, helpful behaviors.

Not all of us were born to live happy lives. Some need a different experience to learn how to find happiness in different circumstances. Some people live their entire existence in grief, anger, gluttony, imperialism, survival, entitlement, jealousy, etc., while searching for comfort from their pain of displeasure. They may not even recognize that they can choose to be happy.

We often see this in people who suffer from war-torn countries, the death of a loved one, the destruction of business, or any other significant loss. They eventually learn and create strategies from their suffering and can teach others how to do so as well. We can further reduce our pain while helping others by simply sharing an inspirational message. As humans, we are RESILIENT. Our release of suffering can help us heal and allow our happiness to emerge.

> ⚡ *Recognize that everyone possesses their own level of happiness. By placing your focus on love, joy, and peace, you will bring happiness into the world.*

In Search of Happiness

We are all entitled to and capable of being happy. Most of us know this yet continue on a never-ending pursuit to find it. Our quest becomes our goal in life. Our past haunts us, and our future stresses us. To cope, we try to cover up our pain with external distractions. As we become consumed in our regrets or worries, we block happiness from emerging.

Just saying we are happy does not necessarily mean we believe it. We must feel a sense of satisfaction in life beyond our physical possessions as these can fade away. Although possessions do not equate to happiness, you can bolster your mental and emotional states to generate contentment through empowering actions, thoughts, and feelings. You will soon find happiness inside by feeling like you have power and control over your life and your decisions.

> ⚡ *Make happiness happen. Your old routines and habits can keep you stuck in the past or fretting about the future. Break them with positive activities and thoughts to generate happiness and contentment.*

One surefire way to generate happiness is through action. You can do this in many ways, including offering THANKS, paying compliments, and investing time with others by having fun, laughing, whistling, or giving back. You know this works because happiness increases your laughter and outward displays of contentment. It is also effective to tap into your memories and virtually relive experiences when you once felt content. Recall times when you smiled so much that your cheeks hurt or even met an exercise goal. These are only a few of many ways to bring out your happiness. Remember, everything you do is for a purpose and will guide you on your path to prosperity and happiness. We are happiest when we are moving forward.

Law of Growth - You will not grow without knowing dissatisfaction. Never be satisfied with your self-growth. Always strive for more self-awareness.

ENJOY Being Love

Love can be so confusing. It has so many meanings and various intensities that people do not know how to identify, get, or keep it. When you love something, you'll tend to gravitate toward it. This attraction may generate feelings of passion, affection, and trust that can lead to commitment, care, and protection. Love offers us such a sense of fulfillment, belonging, and purpose.

For our purposes, we will consider three types of love; physical, emotional, and energetic. All of them are important to us as humans, and each has its unique purpose. The first and simplest form of love is physical. It is biological and stimulates our desires to touch, such as caressing, kissing, sex, holding hands, etc. It is the simplest because it is an instinctual necessity and an innate part of our survival. Its simplicity certainly does not indicate it's not vital. The power of affectionate touch in itself creates a hormone called oxytocin that gives you good feelings and keeps fear and stress low. You seek physical love from your external environment because you do not have that within yourself. Although essential, it is only one form of love and can be more easily controlled by choosing not to act on it.

Physical love can lead to emotional love and vice versa. It's a strong desire or passion based on an attachment to someone, something, or some activity. You may fall in love with your spouse, pets, activities, foods, etc., and have a strong urge to do or have it constantly. You can also love specific thoughts and feelings that offer you a sense of safety, acceptance, and warmth. We all have feelings of love and can express them through our extensions of care. This form of love is the middle of the line and fulfills your wants instead of your needs. People repeatedly look for proof of emotional love; herein lies our quest to find physical evidence that we have the love we desire.

Gary Chapman calls out these intimate expressions of attraction as sex, touch, affirmations, giving, and quality time in his book, *The Five Love Languages*. For some of us, defining love can be much more profound.

#26 prufrock – you don't have to be that lonely, middle-aged person in a state of confusion and isolation. Instead, be the love you want and find the same in another. Moreover, EMBRACE differences that strengthen you both.

Wayne Dyer states it beautifully in his book, *Being in Balance*. "Love is what's left over when falling in love fades away because love is an endless source. Give it away." Find the emotional love inside yourself that you want, and you will project that into the world and attract the same. This feeling is the magical power used in the law of attraction, and it works for everything you want in your life. Once you realize that we are all connected through feelings of love, you will know that we not only belong together as one, but we are also love in and of itself.

Law of Bliss - Love of all brings bliss and wellness.

Self-Love

We all enter into this world as pure love. We initially know nothing else! As we begin our lives, we tend to forget that we are pure love. In our quest to experience life and still feel pleasure, we move away from our natural birthright of being true love and look to fulfill it from other people. The hard truth is that you will not find it in other people if you do not know what it looks like and are not willing to see it in yourself. Knowing love begins with being love.

To 'be love' is different than an expression or feeling of love. It is an actual state of being where you see the beauty and gifts in everything and everyone as they are, especially yourself. Self-love is not selfish or self-centered. Treating yourself kindly, compassionately, and responsibly will help you develop these same skills to extend to others. You will begin to see that we are all doing the best we can in our Zones. You will start to forgive others for their humanness and imperfections. You will open yourself to gratitude for everything and everyone in your life. Moreover, to extend selfless love, you must love and feel compassion for yourself as you would do for things and people in your external world. In the end, you will make space for more of the love you deserve and desire.

> *Serve other people. By caring for others, you tap into your natural loving state. These selfless acts increase your value and bring joy and fulfillment into your life. Be the love you want to have and you'll attract the same.*

Law of Unconditional Love - You transcend your fears when you accept others without judgment or resistance.

ENJOY Being Joy

Just like love and peace, joy is a state of consciousness. That means that you must make a conscious effort to be joyful. True joy is limitless and can only be accessed if you surrender to it. With it comes a sense of well-being, delight, and satisfaction. Even though it's a choice, you can experience joy in many different things, such as playfulness, sheer amazement, profound learning, being authentic, healthy relationships, and utilizing your five senses. They create good vibes and positive energy. Our bodies let us know we are in joy when it releases and distributes dopamine and serotonin throughout our bodies.

> *Surrender to joy. When you do, you'll experience levels of pleasure equal or greater to any euphoric drugs ever made. It's free, healthy, and accessible all of the time.*

If you allow it to enter your heart, pure joy can bring you to tears. I have experienced tears of joy on quite a few occasions. One of the most memorable times was during a music recitals. Cassie, my godchild, was singing in a language foreign to me, and her powerful voice and casual glance my way touched me so deeply that it resonated in my heart and brought tears of joy to my eyes. I may not have understood the words, but I unquestionably recognized the pure joy that overcame me!

Joy is Bliss Regardless

People often wonder what the difference is between joy and happiness. Although similar, they both have distinguishing features. Nobody needs a reason to experience joy, while happiness requires an explanation. You know you are joyful when you're happy for no apparent reason. It is also different in that you can have joy even in difficult times. Many people can experience joy during adversity, but that does not mean they are happy in that moment, nor do they allow the environment to drag them down. Better yet, they remain joyful and balance the problem by seeing all possible viewpoints. Life hands us enough challenges. When we tap into our true or pure joy, we can lessen stress, increase creativity, and ENJOY activities in our *Zone of Potential* through applied logic and reason.

Some people find it difficult to tap into their joy, but it is not as hard as you may think. You can pull it out through laughter, exciting activities, or acting silly. Involve yourself in your community, nature, or family and perform kind gestures - volunteer to do something with your talent for

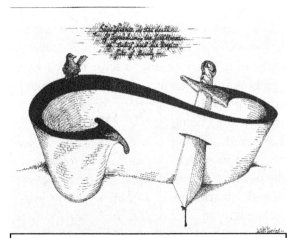

#41 literary symbol – music can touch your soul, but only if you allow it to enter your heart. Choose wisely what you let in!

someone else for free. Connect with someone close to you and offer your assistance. Get out of the house and experience something new, like delicious food, nature, or beautiful scenery. Try learning something hard or finishing a difficult task. You have so many ways to stimulate the joy within you. The key to joy is unconditional kindness to all, including yourself. If joy is what you want, you must intentionally choose it and open yourself up to experience it. As you do, you'll gain more appreciation for what you have, the enormity of the kindness in the world, and a sense of peace through the joy you experience.

ENJOY Being PEACE

When we are constantly on the go, our restless bodies and minds rob us of our inner peace. Without peace, we struggle to ENJOY the moment. We worry a lot and act compulsively on matters that challenge us. As we take on individual problems and absorb the troubles, gossip, and drama of those around us, they fester inside our hearts and heads. Because our worries and judgments are direct reflections of us, we project the same energy into the world. What we receive in return is turmoil, tension, and unease. You have the power to stop all of that and ENJOY life more when you find and EMBRACE the peace within yourself. Once again, you must distinguish it from happiness and consciously bring it into your life, just like love and joy.

#16 flight – you will know you are at peace when you can put yourself out there without fear of what comes back.

You will know when you have peace because you are content, have a sense of balance, and live harmoniously in your surroundings no matter what life throws at you. You are actively involved with life, recognize opportunities, and are open to new experiences. With your new outlook, you become healthier and more RESILIENT. You realize you are doing your best and can only be who you are. No matter what happens, nobody can shake or trouble you when you are at peace. You are present, and feel free.

Peace was one of the most complicated conscious choices for me to EMBRACE. As a person who wants to participate in incredible feats and succeed, I struggled to sit still, listen, and trust my inner messages. The only time I would sit quietly and listen was at home alone or at church which I didn't do very regularly. As a substitute for peace, I would go out for long runs and feel the release of endorphins by the time I finished. Yet most of my activities were an external attempt to find peace. My work inside was not being addressed until I deliberately practiced being present, still, and quiet. Only then was I able to truly be free!

My attempt at inner work was rocky at first. I sat still and did my best to meditate a few times, but I felt like I needed to be doing something. My mind was going 90 miles per hour, and the messages were coming from my to-do list. It all seemed like a waste of my time. Little did I know, through this present quiet stillness, that I would uncover answers to long-held questions. My most profound discovery was my purpose. I also recognize that everything I have done and will do aligns with my desire to express and strengthen my purpose. I learned that nothing is in my way unless I allow it to be. I have the freedom to choose who and what is a part of my life and where to invest my energy. And finally, I can care about everything without an attachment to anything. These messages, and so many more, are how I know I have found peace. With peace in my heart, I can now genuinely extend it to you through this book. You do have peace within yourself, and you deserve to experience it in your Zone and in every ADVENTURE. With peace in mind and heart, be ready to welcome your authentic self.

> *Trust in yourself. You have all of the answers to your questions within. To quickly and easily reveal them, you must be at peace.*

Get Present

People tell others to "get present" like it's an easy thing to do. When, in fact, it is quite the challenge. As we captured in the EMBRACE chapter, Presence in Presents, we know that distractions, interruptions, and multitasking can disrupt peace. Yet, in order to be at peace, we must begin with ourselves and get present.

Amy Cuddy, in her book, *Bring your Boldest Self to Your Biggest Challenges*, looks at presence as "the state of being attuned to and able to comfortably express our true thoughts, feelings, values, and potential." She goes on to say, "It is not a permanent, transcendent mode of being. It comes and goes. It is a moment-to-moment phenomenon." The beauty in her definition is its flexibility for use in our daily lives.

Cherish times of presence and release the tension of constantly needing to have it. If you forcefully attempt to be present, your attention will shift. Your presence will undoubtedly slip away and may cause frustration. With frustration, you will not experience peace at that moment. As Alan Watts states in The Wisdom of Insecurity, "To understand music, you must listen to it. But so long as you are thinking, 'I am listening to this music', you are not listening." Don't chase or overthink it! ENJOY the peace in knowing you were present and will be present again. The point here is to practice getting into the moment whenever you can. Make it intentional and ENJOYABLE by not expecting to be there every minute or even every second of the day.

Being present is different from doing activities to become present, although they indeed complement one another. Being present means tuning in to what is going on inside and around you at that instant. Your physical, emotional, mental, and energetic traits are all part of how you are at any moment. By paying attention to them, you will notice that you are being present. Just keep in mind that once you become aware that you are observing, it's now another moment, and your other thought has passed. Have fun practicing it; you'll notice your senses sharpen even when you're not trying.

Practice Being Present

As you practice being present and tap into each aspect of your physical, mental, emotional, and energetic being, start with your five senses. Then, extend to the following sections: get still, get quiet, and get free. Your five senses offer you an initial external tool to get you present, and the rest will naturally follow. Here are some ways to help you use each of your senses.

Put your complete focus on what you are doing. Look at every aspect of what is in front of you and notice the details. Look around and see how it fits into your surroundings. Observe how your surroundings harmonize with the bigger picture of what you are doing right now. Listen to the moments of silence and each sound within earshot without trying to figure out what it is. When you notice the harmony, EMBRACE the moment of knowing you are perfectly where you should be. Feel the peace and ENJOY. The purpose is to experience the moment and not assign meaning or make an effort to understand anything. Focus on recognizing things for what they are, not what you assume them to be.

Feel everything that is touching you at that moment. It could be your clothing or water or the ground at your feet. Feel the air around you and sense the temperature, moisture, and clarity. Smell without trying to figure out why or what it is. Savor the aromas around you or expand your smells by going outside or opening a window and breathing in the fragrances where you live - delight in the enormity of the world. Feel the peace in knowing that we are one with creation and ENJOY.

Slow your eating and drinking. Let your mouth truly experience your food by pausing to taste each ingredient before swallowing. Taste old favorites and relish in the intricacy of delicious flavors and textures. Invite new savory experiences by trying different treats and swirling them around your mouth. With each flavor-filled bite, know that you are nourishing the vessel structured for your unique purpose. Find peace in your eating and drinking pleasure and ENJOY.

Practicing these presence techniques can be as fun, relaxing, or exciting as you wish. Remember, do not think about or judge what you experience each time you practice. Sense it and discover the pleasure in everything you encounter in each moment. As you do, you will increase your awareness and presence. You will find peace and inner calmness by getting you out of your head, away from your busy thoughts and emotions, and focused more on the present. As a benefit, you will increase your self-awareness, patience, and memory. Once you generate calmness through your senses, you can sit still and develop clearer thoughts about the world around you.

Law of Silence – Wisdom comes in the silence of the mind.

Get Still

Ever since we were kids, we've been told to sit still, quit fidgeting, and calm ourselves down. Yet, with all of the hustle and bustle in our worlds, we still struggle to find time for stillness. Our minds and bodies are constantly on the go. Let's face it, we have places to go, things to do, and people to see. Who really has time to slow down, let alone stop? With all of this over-achieving, we neglect ourselves, stress ourselves out, lose focus of what's important, and hold onto trivial demands. Everything must be correct, on time, and complete before we can finally relax.

If we sit still for a moment, we will see how our accomplishments have positively impacted the world. We would unwind, NURTURE ourselves and our lives a little better, and let up on activities that challenge our core values. We would learn to EMBRACE and ENJOY what we are doing once again. Although life is serious, we sometimes take it too seriously. You

> *Slow down and make room on your calendar to rest and recreate. You will sharpen your vision, discover limitless possibilities, and flourish in creations for a better tomorrow. ENJOY the stillness!*

can slow your roll to stop the ball from spinning, but it must be a conscious choice. Unfortunately, sometimes we forget the things that are truly important to us until we make an effort to rediscover them.

One of the activities you can do is to set time aside to stop physically. When you move around, it's hard to feel the small messages your body is telling you. You might sense aches and pains, but instead of listening to its messages, you will likely make excuses for the discomfort. Usually, it is telling you to stop and rest. This is so true for me. I overused my tendons and ligaments from repetitive exercise routines. I've also strained my eyes, elbow, neck, and shoulders from simply using a computer. We routinely do things to our bodies, and it is constantly lets us know if it likes it or not. By getting still, you can pay attention to it and adjust your activities for a healthier body.

Our bodies also offer us intuitive signals before we do something foolish. For example, many of us were disciplined when we sassed back to our parents. To this day, we may get a gut feeling when we think about doing it as adults. You can think of many, many instances when your intuition told you to stop, but you didn't. You also know that if you had slowed your thoughts and stopped your activity, your outcome likely would have been much more pleasant. Through stillness, you can become more decisive and intentional through clarity and control.

As for our minds, they go so fast and constantly run! Slowing or stopping these is even harder because they never sleep. Even when you sleep, your mind is still busy creating dreams and tapping into subconscious and unconscious thoughts. When you become still and calm your mind, you drastically improve your ability to learn and experience a sense of peace. You will become more present, intentional, and focused yet flexible in your thoughts and actions.

Get Quiet

It's one thing to stop moving and another to stop the noise inside our heads. Your mind constantly moves and never stops. A few research studies floating around claim we have anywhere from 6,000 to upwards of 60,000 thoughts per day. Since thoughts are difficult to measure, we will just assume we have thousands of thoughts per day. It's no wonder we have such a hard time getting a quiet mind. Unfortunately, studies also agree that a large number of thoughts are negative and repetitive. On top of that, much of what we fret over never happens or is easily handled. Of the troublesome worries, most people found that the lessons learned in creating solutions were not worth the trouble or time to figure out.

Darring

#34 meditation – in silence comes awareness. Practice silence and awareness to begin self-growth and end internal conflict!

Although you cannot stop your brain from thinking, you can channel your thoughts. Once you get the hang of it, you can manage most of your thoughts pretty well. Be the teacher of your brain, tell it what to do, and quiet your thoughts. Sometimes you'll still have lingering emotions, such as worry, anger, or sadness. For these thoughts, you can use guided relaxation tools, breathing techniques, or simple journal writing to get them out of your head. Keep working at it, and once you can hear the silence, even for a moment, you'll find your thinking clears, focus sharpens, and reasoning improves. Get quiet and be the peace you desire and deserve.

> *Respect your quiet time and take great care in harnessing the power of silence.*

As you get quiet, you'll feel poised and calm. When you listen to the silence, you'll find it louder, clearer, and more accurate than the noise around you. You will become more alert, alive, and conscious of your decisions and the way you have been living your life. Your moments of silence will provide a space for you to let regrets from your past and worries about your future fade away so you can be PEACEFUL and ENJOY everything here and now.

Get Free

Freedom is a subjective term. People have different ideas about what it means and if they actually have it. We are all born free and become constrained by societal activities, norms, rules, and expectations. These are not necessarily bad or good. To live together harmoniously, some practices can even be quite helpful. Societies have long ago established philosophy, spirituality, religions, and governing bodies to help us learn to co-exist well together. They all work on good intent, but they also can sometimes become extreme and mislead us.

To have freedom is to make decisions based on what you want that is best for you to live your purpose without interfering on others'. You live life fully and give yourself permission to make mistakes, grieve, and take risks. You create your life and have the freedom to shape it any way you desire. You have your own purpose, vision, and mission and are not concerned about what others think about them as long as you accomplish them without infringing on others' freedoms. When any of these are hindered, you may feel like you do not have your freedom. Many people will fight and die for it!

To feel free is to love and accept who you are and tear down limiting beliefs about yourself and your abilities. When you liberate yourself from preconceived notions, convictions, and judgments, you recognize you have the right and power to think and feel in any way you wish without being constrained by anyone. When restrictions are put in place and do not allow you to express your free will, you will feel like you do not have freedom. You may fight yourself or others to defend your right to this feeling of freedom. But hold on because true freedom is not only about having and feeling free – it is about being free.

To be free, you release long-held or unhelpful beliefs and give gracious space for others to do the same. You ENJOY and treasure each moment and do not have much time for meaningless conflicts. You find it easy to be yourself and see others as who they are without judgment or comparison. You are confident in your equality as a human regardless of your role in life. To be truly free, you know that nobody can take your freedom away because it is inside of you. Ultimately, true freedom allows you the peace you deserve, so you can fully ENJOY life as it is, moment by moment, in your *Zone of Potential*.

Chapter 11

Make Life Your Favorite ADVENTURE

W ant to test out the material you just learned? You can start making your life your favorite ADVENTURE by opening up to deeper self-discovery. This chapter is a quick guide – to help you reveal trends in your values, ideals, and behaviors.

The idea is not to do anything ultra life-changing, unless that's your desire. Sometimes even the smallest revelations and actions can impact your life or lead you to VENTURE toward something you can truly ENJOY. You do not have to write anything down, but I find it easier for a couple of reasons. When you write, you incorporate more of your senses (to include taste, if you are snacking). Trends are also easier to identify when you can see them. The same words or phrases may pop out at you and give you insights as to your purpose or passion. So, grab some paper, if you like, and ENJOY!

AWAKEN:

Name ten characteristics about yourself. (Consider your roles, experiences, job positions, hobbies, etc.) Which are your favorites?

Name two issues or unwanted experiences that continue to pop up. What are they trying to tell you? (Consider finances, health, partnered relationships, family, friends, jobs, recreation, home, etc.)

Name the things you have most of in your surroundings. How does each fit into how you see yourself? What works and what doesn't? (Consider your books, tools, games, beauty, pictures, equipment, clothing, etc.)

Name one thing in your life where you are very organized. What did you do with it the last time you touched it?

Name only five things you would take if you had to suddenly move, get a new job, or go on vacation. How would that list change if you were evacuated? Why would you leave the rest behind?

Name three things you would purchase if you only had $5. What helped you choose?

Name two of your best friends. Why did you choose them?

Name three activities you would not change in your daily routine. How did you decide on them?

Name three people you would go to for advice. What's the best advice you've ever received?

Name two people who have had the most significant influence on your life. How did they influence you?

Name one of your favorite hobbies, games, or activities you love to do for hours. How does it relate to your personal and professional work?

Name five of your best personality traits. What makes these your favorite?

Name two positive physical aspects of yourself. How do you see them in your personal and professional areas of life? How does your inner self reflect your physical self?

Name an event that you were completely against doing, yet you were glad you did it when it was over. Why were you hesitant to go? How did it affect your life or willingness to try new things?

Name one thing you are doing or not doing that goes against your values. How is it limiting your ability to have a fulfilled life?

Name three new experiences over the past five years that significantly impacted your life. What effect have they left on your life today? What were any specific lessons you learned through the process?

Name two things you have considerably improved on over the last ten years. If these are ongoing endeavors, do you want to stay the course, or is it time to shift your efforts? List the possible pros and cons of your choices.

DANCE:

Name one physical, mental, or emotional activity you do so well that people ask for your help or advice. How do you feel when asked?

Name one thing you want to take over when you see people doing it wrong. What does that tell you about yourself?

Name three things you expect others intuitively to know, feel, or be able to do but, instead, people often miss the mark. How would you be able to help?

Name two topics you ENJOY deeper learning from books, reading material, or instructional videos. What pulls you toward them?

Name one topic you cannot seem to get enough information about. What does this reveal to you?

Name one thing or person you can tap into to hone your talent and use it wisely. What guided you to choose it?

Name one person who shares the same knowledge interest as you. How do you interact with that person? (face-to-face, online, writing, texting, etc.). Also, during your interaction, how do you actively listen, argue, interrupt, finish sentences, etc.?

VENTURE:

Name a vision of how you would want people to remember you. What steps would be involved? How will you know you are inspired or committed enough to invest your time and energy to accomplish that vision?

Name two activities you infrequently do to support your vision. How could you include that into your regular daily or weekly routine?

Name three things holding you back from creating your mission (the steps) to support your vision. What effect is that having on you?

Name one thing that inspires (pulls you) you to make that vision come true. How do you feel when you think about it?

Name three opportunities available to you to carry out your vision. What external barriers hold you back?

Name three small activities that will make your vision come alive. How does this make your vision more manageable?

Name one small step you are willing to take right now toward your vision. What other opportunities will your one step create?

Name two important issues that require focused attention right now. What's standing in your way of resolving them?

Name three current barriers (success, failure, size, complexity, difficulty, etc.) that keep you in fear. What would happen if you faced them?

Name and complete one achievable goal. Keep it simple, easy to complete, aligned with your vision, and in a realistic timeframe. What do you have in place now to help achieve it?

Name a goal you achieved in the last six months. What did this goal achievement allow you to do next?

EMBRACE:

Name one memory of people, things, or events in your past that you believe are holding you back. What barriers still exist that keep you stuck?

Name one regret of a past decision you hold onto that has you stuck. How would you feel if you left that regret behind and stepped forward in your life without it?

Name three opportunities you seized during your lifetime that you were prepared to take. What were you able to learn from them?

Name three opportunities you ignored in your life. What held you back? Name one unfortunate circumstance you experienced that opened opportunities for you. What positive outcome came from it?

Name three distractions and interruptions you are giving into on a daily basis. What is that telling you about your values or priorities? If nothing, what are you trying to avoid or escape?

Name one activity you perform that requires total concentration. What is it like to complete it?

Name five qualities you have that can help you live a fulfilling life. What value do these qualities bring?

Name two people with whom you compare yourself. How are those comparisons helping or hurting you?

Name one worry you have about your future. How is it holding you back?

Name three simple pleasures you ENJOY. What makes them pleasureful? What pain does it relieve?

NURTURE:

Name two healthy areas in your life and two that need more attention. How can you harmonize the four? (Consider your diet, exercise, work, rest, relationships, money, pets, etc.)

Name one activity you usually do that you can intensify to improve your health. How will this affect other areas of your life? (walk, house cleaning or maintenance, bike, shop, yard work, etc.)

Name one day of the week you are willing to schedule a nap if you are not getting enough rest. How will you know it is helping you?

Name one of your favorite hobbies. What does it do for you?

Name one way you can include others in your hobby. How will that bring harmony into your life?

Name one time of the day to sit and breathe deeply and completely from your belly for five minutes. As you breathe, what feelings do you get, and what thoughts come up for you?

Name one way you can practice kindness to those close to you and others in your environment. How will that improve your relationships with people, things, and activities?

Name two small things in your home or work that you can improve. How do you feel when you finish?

Name three things you will give away that no longer serve you. What feelings come up for you?

THANK:

Name two hard lessons from your childhood that shaped what you do today. Looking back, what are you grateful for in overcoming that experience?

Name one person who offended you in the past. What did you learn about yourself through the experience?

Name one fun time with a childhood friend. What did you learn that adds value to your life today?

Name one catastrophe on earth. What were any of the positive stones that came out of the event?

Name one mistake that embarrassed you. What did the error teach you about yourself?

Name one person in your life who upsets you. What will it take to forgive them and release that energy?

Name one of your personal or professional qualities that you are prepared to share more with others. How have you done this in the past, or how will you begin?

Name one thing you never had that you want to own or one activity you have never done but want to accomplish. What would the experience do for you?

Name one thing you wondered about others that mysteriously showed up for you. When did you finally realize it?

Name two ways you will know you are on the right track to do or receive what you want from life. What feelings will you get when you have it?

UPLIFT:

Name one negative aspect you believe to be true about yourself that affects your life. What benefit might there be of having it?

Name two negative thoughts, feelings, or beliefs you have about others. What do those people do well?

Name one statement someone said about you. How did that drive you to develop yourself?

Name one mistake you continue to recall (different from the previous). How did that help you shape your life?

Name five things in your surroundings that are valuable to you. How do they bring joy into your life?

Name a group you joined. What are the positive and negative aspects of the group?

Name a country you do not want to visit. What are some positive qualities of that country?

Name your culture and a culture with which you feel you don't belong. What are the similarities between yours and theirs?

RESILIENCE:

Name three commitments you have made in your lifetime. What enabled you to continue to fulfill those commitments?

Name two things you've quit. What drove you to start and stop?

Name three things you committed to doing yet shifted to other activities. What was your deciding factor?

Name an event when you felt like a complete failure. What positive messages can you take away from the experience now?

Name one accomplishment where you were thoroughly prepared and still made mistakes. What positive lessons can you take away from it?

Name three people who consistently helped you physically, mentally, and emotionally. What is it that they do to help you?

Name your favorite tool or piece of equipment. What makes it your favorite? What value does it bring you?

Name two investments you have made in your self-development over the last five years. What prompted you to choose those?

Name the last time you forgot what you were looking for. What were you thinking about instead?

Name two people who are no longer involved in your life. What is the benefit of them going their separate ways? What is the likelihood that you would reach out to them again?

Name one area of your life where everything seems like it flows easily. How does it feel, and how can you replicate that in other areas of your life?

ENJOY:

Name one activity you are happy to do that other people aren't. What about it makes you happy?

Name five traits you love about each parent or guardian. Which traits do you have, and who else has them in your life?

Name joyful events in your life in which you participate. What about them brings you joy?

Name one way you can still and quiet your thoughts. What does that allow you to do?

Name three ways you are free in your life. What possibilities does that freedom allow you to experience?

As you reflect on what you uncover and answer the questions above, you begin to AWAKEN to whom you have become. With a greater understanding of yourself, your DANCE will emerge. You may find yourself feeling compelled to VENTURE into new experiences. As you do, EMBRACE where your past has brought you and begin from there. NURTURE yourself and take care of the people and things along your path who bring you value and joy. UPLIFT yourself by knowing you are fully capable of doing what you intend to do. Extend the same to others and determine if there are ways for you to help them reach their goals. As the reality of your desires unfolds, just remember you have the power of intuition to determine whether what you are doing is appropriate for you. As you commit to your vision, resource yourself with the best mindset, tools, and people who want to see you succeed. With this support, you will be RESILIENT to challenges, creatively tackle issues that may arise, and maintain a sense of control, so that you can stay the course. With this in mind, be sure to ENJOY a life of peace through love, joy, and happiness along each ADVENTURE. From Alpha to Omega, beginning to end, and AWAKEN to ENJOY, you are the creator of your life, one ADVENTURE at a time!

References

Allen, J. (2016). As a Man Thinketh: The Passionpreneur University Edition. (n.p.): CreateSpace Independent Publishing Platform.

Bogle, J. C. (2010). Enough: True Measures of Money, Business, and Life. (pp. 192) Switzerland: Wiley.

Buckingham, M., Coffman, C. (2014). First, Break All the Rules: What the World's Greatest Managers Do Differently. (pp. 31) United States: Gallup Press.

Chapman, G. (2004). The Five love languages. Northfield.

Collier, R. (2007). The secret of the ages. (pp. 162) Jeremy P. Tarcher/Penguin.

Covey, S. M. R. (2008). The Speed of Trust: The One Thing that Changes Everything. United Kingdom: Simon & Schuster UK.

Csikszentmihalyi, M. (2009). Flow: The psychology of optimal experience. Harper and Row.

Cuddy, A. (2015). Presence: Bringing Your Boldest Self to Your Biggest Challenges. United States: Little, Brown.

Desy, Phylameana Lila. "Five Layers of the Human Energy Field." Learn Religions, Aug. 26, 2020, learnreligions.com/layers-of-human-energy-field-1729677.

Dispenza, D. R. J. O. E. (2019). In Becoming supernatural: How common people are doing the uncommon (pp. 111–111). essay, HAY House UK LTD.

Dotchamou, Z (2018). 270 Life Changing Quotes from Jim Rohn (n.p.): Lulu.com.

Dyer, W. W. (2009). Being in Balance: 9 Principles for Creating Habits to Match Your Desires: Easyread Large Bold Edition. (n.p.): Createspace Independent Pub.

Gallup., Buckingham, M., Clifton, D. O. (2001). Now, Discover Your Strengths. (pp. 25, 41) United Kingdom: Gallup Press.

Harper, H. (2019, January 29). 6 ways to overcome the forgetting curve. Chartwell Content. Retrieved February 6, 2022, from https://chartwellcontent.com/idea/2019/1/17/6-ways-to-overcome-the-forgetting-curve

Hendry, E. (2013, November 20). 7 Epic Fails Brought to You By the Genius Mind of Thomas Edison. Smithsonian.

Kaku, M. (2019). The Future of Humanity: Our Destiny in the Universe. United States: Knopf Doubleday Publishing Group.

Killingsworth, M. A., & Gilbert, D. T. (2010). A wandering mind is an unhappy mind. Science, 330(6006), 932–932. https://doi.org/10.1126/science.1192439

Mark, G., Gonzalez, V. M., & Harris, J. (2005). No task left behind? Proceedings of the SIGCHI Conference on Human Factors in Computing Systems. https://doi.org/10.1145/1054972.1055017

Maxwell, J. C. (2007). Failing Forward. United States: Thomas Nelson Incorporated.

Nobuhiro, H., Haggard, P., and Diedrichsen, J. (2017). Perceptual decisions are biased by the cost to act. eLife. doi:10.7554/eLife.18422

Rohn, E. J. (2019). In Seven strategies for wealth and happiness (pp. 67–67). essay, Manjul Publishing House.

Schwartz, D. J. (2014). The Magic of Thinking Big. United States: Penguin Publishing Group.

The Mystical Books Plus. (2022, February 20). 50 universal laws that affect our reality ... - youtube.com. Retrieved March 1, 2022, from https://www.youtube.com/watch?v=h6em1nutfjg

Watts, A. (1951). The Wisdom of Insecurity. (pp. 87) United Kingdom: Pantheon.

A Special Tribute to Walter Darring

Artist, Poet, Professor, and most lucky title of all, Uncle

This tribute to my Uncle Walt, "Sonny", "Bapu" is a special yet unexpected one. For almost 40 years, his book of art collections, "*the eyeful tower*", traveled with me throughout my military career and beyond. It went from duty station to duty station and home to home. Who would have thought this amazing gem of a book I swiped from my father in 1983 and sat on my shelf for about 4 decades would contain art perfectly designed for my book, "***Zone of Potential***"?

I may not believe in coincidences or luck, but I do believe in synchronicity. Things are supposed to fall into place at the time and in the order most suitable for each one of our ADVENTURES. The time it took for the editors, artists, and publishing to come together offered me a unique opportunity to pay tribute to a fine artist, poet, professor, and most of all, special uncle!

Oblivious of the treasure trove sitting on my shelf, I continued to write and consider illustrations that would best represent the book's content. I mulled over using real-life photos of my experiences as a personal touch, but that idea felt flat. I also contacted a long-time friend, colleague, and talented artist, Wade Forbes, to see if he would hand-draw some illustrations. He graciously accepted. We delayed a few times as neither one of us was quite ready.

Unbeknownst to me, Uncle Sonny, or "Bapu", was in his last few days, preparing for his peaceful passage to join his wife and true love, Aunt Jean, in heaven. The night before he passed, I received a text from John, Uncle Sonny's son and my cousin. He informed me of Bapu's health and the expectation of him passing within 24 hours. I was greatly saddened and took out his book to reflect on his life and our relationship.

As I leafed through Uncle Sonny's drawings, I noticed that every illustration in his book, "***the eyeful tower***" reflected the messages in my book "*Zone of Potential.*" Suddenly, a surge of energy shot through me. Although I delayed reaching out to my cousin out of respect and timing, eventually, I gently requested permission to honor Uncle Sonny through a lovely tribute in my book and sprinkle some of his art in fitting places. John welcomed the idea and happily checked into my request with other family members. After a few weeks, I received the message from cousin John - GRANTED!! I suddenly found myself in tears of joy!

I am honored, grateful, and humbled to have this opportunity to merge 33 of Uncle Sonny's drawings from his book "*the eyeful tower*" as a visual expression of my book, "*Zone of Potential.*" Uncle Sonny will always be known to many as a happy, talented, and fun-loving man. He is a true representation of how people can make life their favorite ADVENTURE. A special thanks to cousin John for contacting me and my cousins, who graciously allowed me to feature Bapu's art and honor him through this tribute.

Uncle Sonny, your love, smile, and infectious laughter will forever be in my heart and thoughts. You always have been and forever will be my "Sonny side." May you rest in peace with your wife (Jean), my mother (Charlotte), and all of the beautiful souls who passed before you.

With much love and gratitude,

Karin

ABOUT THE AUTHOR

*K*arin Schultz has always been fascinated by human behavior. Her magnetic draw began during her childhood as part of a large family and transitioned to her many roles as a US Marine and government civilian. As she pursued her Bachelor's degree in business and her Master's degrees in cyber and business, she noticed her persistent draw to the behavioral aspects delivered in each curriculum. After retirement from government service, Karin decided it was time to share her leadership experience, extensive training, and personal development through *Zone of Potential*, a coaching and consulting business and now a book.

Karin lives in Maryland with her husband, John and treasures every opportunity to be with her daughter and stepson as they navigate their lives. You will often catch Karin participating in various recreational activities, learning something new, and most of all, enjoying her favorite ADVENTURE, life! Come join Karin in her quest to bring peace, joy, love, and happiness to all through her sense of ADVENTURE.

Live life like it is your favorite

ADVENTURE!

Zone of Potential

Make Life Your Favorite ADVENTURE

"The Zone of Potential guided me through an insightful examination of my life. Karin's expert advice encouraged me to reevaluate what were truly the most important facets of my life and how to redirect my energies towards them. Most surprisingly, I also realized that I would continue to struggle to fulfill my goals if I did not start to practice self-care, nourishing both mind and body. Karin's intellect, wisdom, and logical approach should serve to galvanize 10,000s of readers to reassess their lives and prepare to embrace the new adventures which wait them." - Alice Hoey, Professor

"Through Karin's teachings, personal stories, and tie-in with the universal laws, she challenges you to think deeper and really evaluate your life and what you are doing. I can promise you, when you read this book and start implementing Karin's ADVENTURE guide, your Zone of Potential will reveal itself so you can commit to what you want next and create an amazingly adventurous life." - Kelly Falardeau, Award Winning Virtual Speaker and 7x Bestselling Author

To learn more about Karin Schultz and Zone of Potential
Scan the QR code above or visit my website.
www.zoneofpotential.com

If you enjoyed Zone of Potential
Please post a review on Amazon at www.amazon.com

ISBN 979-8-21-802491-8

9 798218 024918 >

Made in the USA
Middletown, DE
18 July 2022